The Observer's Pocket Series

FLY FISHING

Observer's Books

NATURAL HISTORY
Birds · Bird's Eggs · Wild Animals · Zoo Animals
Farm Animals · Freshwater Fishes · Sea Fishes
Tropical Fishes · Butterflies · Larger Moths
Insect and Spiders · Pond Life · Sea and Seashore
Seashells · Dogs · Horses and Ponies · Cats
Trees · Wild Flowers · Grasses · Mushrooms · Lichens
Cacti · Garden Flowers · Flowering Shrubs
House Plants · Vegetables · Geology · Weather
Astronomy

SPORT
Association Football · Cricket · Golf · Coarse Fishing
Fly Fishing · Show Jumping · Motor Sport

TRANSPORT
Automobiles · Aircraft · Commercial Vehicles
Motorcycles · Steam Locomotives · Ships
Small Craft · Manned Spaceflight · Unmanned
Spaceflight

ARCHITECTURE
Architecture · Churches · Cathedrals

COLLECTING
Awards and Medals · Coins · Postage Stamps
Glass · Pottery and Porcelain

ARTS AND CRAFTS
Music · Painting · Modern Art · Sculpture
Furniture · Sewing

HISTORY AND GENERAL INTEREST
Ancient Britain · Flags · Heraldry · European Costume

TRAVEL
London · Tourist Atlas GB

The Observer's Book of
FLY FISHING

PETER WHEAT

DRAWINGS BY BAZ EAST

WITH 8 COLOUR PLATES, 23 BLACK AND
WHITE PHOTOGRAPHS AND NUMEROUS
DIAGRAMS IN THE TEXT

FREDERICK WARNE

LONDON

Published by
Frederick Warne (Publishers) Ltd
London, England
1977

ISBN 0 7232 1561 8

Printed in Great Britain by
William Clowes & Sons Limited
London, Beccles and Colchester
2555·377

Preface

The sport of fly fishing is ancient but definitely not old-fashioned. It has moved with the times and continues to attract a great many new converts every season. This is a book of practical fly-fishing instruction, and is intended as initial guidance for newcomers of all ages to this absorbing pastime.

To provide scope for further study of specialized aspects a list of books for further reading has been included on pages 173–5. Also at the back of the book will be found details of a selection of day-ticket trout waters in England and Wales.

Acknowledgement is due to the following for the illustrations in this book: Bill Howes, Brian Bates, Bob Church, Al Pond and Ray Forsberg for colour photographs; L. S. Paterson (front endpaper), Roy Westwood (p. 20), Fred J. Taylor (pp. 37, 149 both), Irish Tourist Board (pp. 42, 124 and back endpaper), Peter Rayment (pp. 56, 131), Angling Times (p. 83), George Armit (p. 113), Bill Howes (p. 142) and Bob Church (p. 152) for black and white photographs other than my own. I should especially like to thank my close friend, Baz East, for drawings in the text.

I must also acknowledge the generous assistance of the publisher's staff, at all stages, and my wife, Margaret, who was endlessly patient during the weeks I hid myself in 'The Den' writing the manuscript.

Lastly, grateful thanks to the fly-fishing masters of all ages past and present. I feel their influence with each cast I make, and appreciate well that the fish I catch are as much theirs as mine.

Peter Wheat

Contents

List of Colour Plates

Introduction

Fly fishing was already long established and much practised when the first book in the English language on the subject of angling was published in 1492. Entitled *A Treatyse of Fyshynge with an Angle*, ascribed to Dame Juliana Berners, and printed at Westminster as part of the second edition of *The Boke of St Albans*, this work describes the rod and line of fly fishing at that early date, and suggests in a list of 12 wet flies dressings easily recognizable as imitations of such well-known insects as March Brown, Olive Dun, Great Red Spinner, Stone Fly, Sedge Fly and Alder Fly.

These flies were intended to be dapped across the water on horsehair lines fixed to the tips of enormous 18–20 ft (5·4–6 m) 'rod-poles', so clearly it was important during those embryo days of fly fishing to go forth only in breezy weather when gusty winds could billow the line and the insect imitation far out over the water, preferably in a downstream direction.

Tackle, flies and this method remained virtually unchanged for the next 150 years, but from then on a steady influx of new ideas and fresh attitudes slowly but inevitably transformed fly fishing from a primitive simplicity to its present-day complexity. Upstream fishing, casting (as opposed to dapping), and heavier tapered lines of horsehair and horsehair and silk, all came in during the 17th century; reels, running lines, and rods of reduced length, towards the close of the 18th century; dry-fly fishing in the 19th century, and nymph fishing at the beginning of the 20th century.

Nowadays, fly fishing is more popular than ever before, and the ranks of enthusiasts increase with the passing of each year—strengthened by both complete novices to angling and seasoned coarse and sea fishermen seeking a change of scene or additional variety.

The sacrosanct aura which lingered long from the Grand Cult of the Dry Fly, fashionable on lush chalkstreams at the turn of the century, has now all but disappeared. And so too has the biased attitude of that narrow-minded section of English anglers who did not fly fish and who thought of trout as stupid beasts fit only as quarry for the idle rich.

Trout are now generally regarded as first-class sport by all sections of angling. And fly fishing, once shrouded in mystery and held in awe by the populace, has been exposed as a method, indeed a whole approach to catching fish, which can be undertaken by anybody of any age from 12 upwards—even younger in some cases.

This, then, is a book for newcomers who are yet to catch their first rod-and-line fish, and anglers from other branches of the sport exploring the possibilities of fly fishing for the first time. I have endeavoured throughout to keep the text simple and basic, and by so doing provide the reader with a foundation of understanding on which to build greater knowledge and specialized interests.

It has been found necessary to generalize, and generalizations are never entirely satisfactory in an activity such as angling, where the particular circumstances of a given moment are the controlling factors and indicate where and how the fly or bait should be presented. These generalizations make sense only when it is realized that they are *first steps* leading to in-depth study coupled with practical experience.

The American angler and writer E. R. Hewitt suggested three stages through which anglers pass. First, a need to catch the greatest possible number of fish; then a growing desire for larger and larger fish; and finally, a passion for catching only the most difficult fish irrespective of numbers or size.

Anglers in the first category mentioned can do no better than seek their trout in wild waters such as the acid streams and lakes of Scotland, Ireland, northern England and the West Country, where brown trout are natural-grown, numerous, and more often than not, hungry, eager feeders. There are also grayling, bleak, dace, rudd and perch to catch from other waters where they are abundant.

Anglers in the second category might well visit a noted sea trout stream at a time of the year when the big fish are running, and there try for them at night in famous pools. With exceptions such as the Hampshire Avon, sea trout are found in rivers where resident browns are small. The largest of the migrating stock, fresh from sea-feeding, are hefty creatures weighing well over the 10 lb (4·5 kg) mark.

Alternatively, the limestone lakes of Ireland may be dapped with natural insects at mayfly time, or later in the year when crane flies fall upon the water, in confident expectation of hooking specimen-size brown trout.

However, for the majority, the 'bread and butter' of lunker-trout hunting is the sport of reservoirs and lakes, where rainbows predominate, but where both rainbows and browns can be taken to weights in excess of 10 lb (4·5 kg). These waters, the principal waters of modern-day trouting, provide as a reward of effort, catches of many fish and, as stimulating bonus, occasional bigger fish.

And elsewhere there are pike to catch—the pike of lakes where they breed in large numbers but remain small by pike standards. A 5–10 lb (2·25–4·5 kg) class pike may not rate as 'big' when hooked on straightforward bottom tackle, but it is certainly 'big' as far as fly fishing is concerned.

Anglers in the third category have more than enough challenges to test their mature skills, with the trout of chalkstream 'dry-fly only' and 'dry fly or upstream nymph' preserves an outstanding speciality. In these choice waters, restricted completely to upstream tactics, there is need for absolutely accurate, carefully measured presentation —setting flies over trout which rise from every conceivable position in the stream. To cast kneeling, from behind a tree, from a confined space—and always, but always, without scaring the quarry even a little. In my opinion, this is fly fishing of a very high order indeed. However, perhaps this is no more intriguing a proposition to open-minded anglers than fly fishing for carp, barbel or large pike!

From my constant references to coarse fish as well as trout, readers will already have gleaned that I am far from being a 'trout-only' angler. I seek coarse, game and sea fish with equal enthusiasm—believing all species and all methods to be of value and interest. But, though I employ fly-tactics for coarse and sea fish as well as trout, and never restrict myself to fly-only for trout if conditions indicate (and rules permit) bait or spinner as methods more likely to succeed, I have no doubt that if forced to restrict myself to just one method and one fish for the rest of my life, I would choose to fly-fish for trout.

My decision would have much to do with the utter fascination of fly-lore: the casting out and the retrieving of flies in the multitude of ways possible, the study of tackle and of natural flies and their imitation on the hook, and the overcoming of crafty fish in adverse circumstances. But nevertheless, I must admit that I would find it difficult to explain my choice completely.

I recall standing on the bank of a lonely reservoir high up in the Breconshire hills one late summer's evening and admiring with intense satisfaction three beautifully marked trout lying on the wet stones of the shoreline. It had rained heavily all day. I was cold and soaked to the skin. And the fish averaged barely half a pound (226 g). Yet I remember feeling as happy then as at any moment in my life.

Is it any wonder that the mystical appeal of catching trout on artificial fly is so impossible to explain—that the only way of truly understanding it is to experience it for yourself?

Man's life is but vain, for 'tis subject to pain
　　And sorrow and short as a bubble;
'Tis a hodge-podge of business and money and care
　　And care and money and trouble.

But we'll take no care when the weather proves fair,
　　Nor will we now vex though it rain;
We'll banish all sorrow, and sing till tomorrow,
　　And angle and angle again.

Anon. c. 1620

Sea trout, *Salmo trutta*

1: TROUT

Of the many species of fish caught on artificial fly, trout, *Salmo trutta* and *Salmo gairdneri*, are by far the best known and most popular with British anglers.

S. trutta, the sea trout and its variety the brown trout, is indigenous as it colonized this area of the world shortly after the retreat of the last major Ice Age some 10,000 years ago.

S. gairdneri, the rainbow trout, is in comparison a newcomer to Britain, having first been introduced in 1884 from North America. It is native to streams entering the Pacific Ocean from Alaska to northern Mexico and the upper parts of the Athabasca river drainage in Alberta, Canada. The rainbow is currently a far more important species in Britain than the brown, in terms of both food and sporting value.

Sea Trout and Brown Trout

The sea trout has a steel-silver black-spotted coloration similar to that of its near relative the Atlantic salmon, *Salmo salar*. And like *S. salar* it spawns in fresh water and moves into salt water for periods of growth.

14

Sea trout ascend sea-connected river systems between spring and autumn. The timing of the main run is locally variable, being greatly influenced from one river to the next by seasonal differences. It may commence as early as April or as late as autumn. Also, there are months when only smaller fish enter a specific river and other months when the bigger fish move up.

Local up-to-date information is vital to successful sea trout fishing.

Unlike salmon, which tend not to feed once in fresh water, sea trout continue feeding at regular intervals after leaving the sea. This habit, together with their greater numbers, makes them easier to catch than salmon—particularly on artificial flies.

Serious sea trout fishing is frequently undertaken at night, with the period between dusk and 2 a.m. considered the likeliest time to expect fish.

The spawning of sea trout occurs during the last quarter of the year. The female scours a saucer-shaped nest, called a redd, in gravel, and into this depression extrudes eggs (ova), which are immediately enveloped with milt (sperm) released by attendant males. The eggs are then hidden by action of the female, tail-sweeping gravel into the trough from an upstream position. Sea trout return to the sea when spawning is completed.

Successfully fertilized eggs hatch during the first quarter of the new year, at about the time winter is giving way to spring. The alevins, as baby trout are

Trout alevin with yolk-sac

called, remain hidden beneath the gravel for between five and six weeks, feeding on nourishment obtained from yolk-sacs attached to their bodies.

Eventually they struggle to the surface of the river bed and commence to feed through the mouth on microscopic forms of aquatic life, developing over the next two or three years first into colourful parrs and then into silvery black-spotted smolts. At this stage of maturity they are ready to begin their journey to the sea.

Migrating smolts move downstream to the estuary and pause there in the brackish environment while complex internal adjustments take place. Equipped at last for sea-living, they swim away from the shore to fatten-up on a diet of such nourishment as shellfish, sand-eels and brit.

Sea trout smolts, unlike salmon smolts, do not travel very far offshore, and by late summer or early autumn, after only a few months in marine conditions, some of them will return to the river of their birth with the incoming spawning shoals. The process of spawning takes place all over again, and the smolts accompany the spawned-out sea trout out to sea again afterwards.

A year later, these fish, with fish of the same stock which did not make the earlier trip, enter fresh water as spawners in their own right and continue to do so each following year until death overtakes them.

Spawned-out sea trout, called kelts, are thin flabby creatures, but they do not suffer the high mortality of salmon kelts, probably because periodic feeding while in fresh water gives them additional strength which is lacking in salmon.

Sea trout grow to weights in excess of 20 lb (9 kg). The larger specimens are difficult to distinguish from salmon.

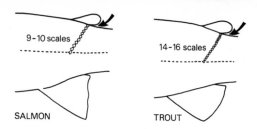

9-10 scales

14-16 scales

SALMON

TROUT

Salmon and trout can be told apart by counting the scales in an oblique series between the back edge of the adipose fin and the lateral line

The brown trout is a non-migratory variety of the sea trout which passes the whole of its life in fresh water. It is an extremely adaptable fish capable of existing successfully in a wide range of environments: streams, rivers, ponds, reservoirs and lakes—including lakes as massive as the sea-like loughs and lochs of Ireland and Scotland.

Being so generally distributed, the brown trout is subject to much variation in growth-rate and in the patterning of its body colours. In the past, these differences led to a mistaken belief that *S. trutta* was not just one species but many separate species.

In old works of reference mention is made of such

Brown trout, *Salmo trutta*

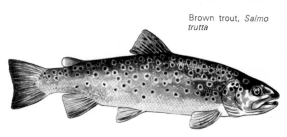

17

fish as the Loch Leven trout, the Welsh black-finned trout, the gillaroo trout, and the great lake trout, etc.—each one identified by its own scientific name. However, it has now long been realized that these 'species' are really nothing more than brown trout strains, that the brown trout is in its turn a variety of the sea trout, and that all of them are, strictly speaking, *S. trutta*.

The extent of variation makes it quite impossible to describe any typical colour pattern for brown trout. There are nearly always spots present, thickly or sparsely sprinkled over the head, body and fins, but the colours of the spots (black, brown and red), and indeed the colours of the flanks and underparts (basically silver or gold shading white or cream beneath), differ to a remarkable degree from one water to the next. In a lake of vast circumference and depth, trout even differ according to the separate zones of the water they inhabit.

Despite all this, brown trout as a group can easily be told apart from other fish. They have a streamlined shape, a long rakish mouth armed with tiny sharp teeth along the edge of the jaws and on the vomer (a bone located in the roof of the mouth), and a common arrangement of fins. These include a fleshy stub on the back between the dorsal fin and the truncated caudal fin known as the adipose fin— typical to all members of the Salmonidae family.

Male trout with kyped
lower jaw

Older male trout develop an upturned hook to the lower jaw called the kype. The purpose of this growth is mainly connected with breeding activities.

In waters where browns are naturally abundant the average size of them is usually small, but what these 'lesser' trout lack in size they make up for in their eagerness to take the flies and baits of the angler. Inhabiting such a fiercely competitive world they can ill-afford to be too choosy about what they will and will not eat, and this being so, they provide grand sport—even though the largest of any day's catch may not weigh more than 1 lb (0·4 kg).

Richer waters breed larger-growing browns, fish weighing between 1 lb (0·4 kg) and 10 lb (4·5 kg), and certain of the big lakes contain 'monsters' approaching, and even exceeding, 20 lb (9 kg). Loughs Erne, Corrib and Mask, of Ireland, are famous for rod-caught trout of double-figure calibre, and on the 6th April 1974, it was Lower Lough Erne which produced an outstanding specimen to the rod of Tom Chartres which pulled the pointer of the weighing scales to 19 lb 4½ oz (8·7 kg).

Scottish lochs also hold giant trout. In 1965, K. J. Grant took a beautifully proportioned specimen from Loch Garry which tipped the scales at 18 lb 2 oz (8·2 kg). A trout from Loch Awe caught in ancient times is reputed to have weighed no less than 39 lb 8 oz (180 kg).

Almost all rod-caught browns weighing 10 lb (4·5 kg) plus have fallen for spoons, spinners and plugs—more frequently in recent years angled on special deep-trolling lure rigs originating from the United States. These leviathans, confirmed deep-water fish-eaters, are unlikely to be encountered when using normal fly-fishing methods and therefore can be discounted for the purpose of this book.

Brian Capener displays his superb 12 lb 5 oz (5·5 kg) Grafham Water brown trout (*Roy Westwood*)

It must be added though, that in a few of the reservoirs restricted to fly fishing there are brown trout present weighing more than 10 lb (4·5 kg) which do occasionally fall victim to artificial fly. In May 1975, Brian Bates caught an 11 lb 5½ oz (5 kg) brown from Cambridgeshire's Grafham Water on a large lure pattern worked near the bottom in 30 ft (9 m) of water. The same fishery yielded an even bigger brown of 12 lb 5 oz (5·5 kg) during May of the following year to the rod of Brian Capener— taken on a size 12 black buzzer drifted on a floating line from the dam wall.

Brown trout spawn during the autumn, and the development of the egg to the adult fish is very similar to that of sea trout—apart from the obvious difference that brown trout never enter the sea. Brown trout in lakes move into tributary streams to spawn, if such inlets exist.

The term 'slob trout' refers to trout which move

into estuary water seeking richer feed and there remain, neither entering the sea nor moving back to the river.

Rainbow Trout

The rainbow trout is commonly stocked in fisheries all over the country as the principal sporting species. Like the brown trout it is a tough fighter, but an even more spectacular adversary on the hook because of the leaping antics in which it indulges.

The body shape of *S. gairdneri* is very similar to that of *S. trutta*, but rainbow coloration is distinctive enough to tell the two species apart. The back and upper flanks are olive-gold with subdued hints of blue, the lower flanks silver shading white beneath. Along the middle of the flanks of mature fish runs a horizontal flush of red or pink (hence the name rainbow) which is at its most pronounced during the breeding season. Spotting consists of dark freckles.

In Britain, rainbow trout do not breed very successfully in the wild. They experience difficulty in shedding their eggs, and eggs which are dropped and fertilized fail to hatch. Now and then a length of river or a lake yields a batch of wild-bred rainbows,

Rainbow trout, *Salmo gairdneri*

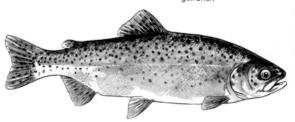

but at present the only established indigenous domains in this country are the river Chess of Buckinghamshire and the lower six miles (10 km) of the Derbyshire Wye, together with its tributary stream the Lathkil.

Shortly before the close of the last century, 400 rainbows were stocked in a lake at Ashford, not far from the Wye. A period of high water and subsequent flooding enabled some of these fish to leave the lake and enter the river. They settled the Wye with a vengeance, breeding prolifically and severely reducing the native brown trout and grayling populations as they spread downstream towards Rowsley, where the Wye enters the Derwent. Today, rainbow trout dominate this stretch and sections of the Lathkil, and I am told they outnumber the brown trout 20 to 1.

In nearly all trout waters rainbows are stocked on a 'put and take' basis. That is to say, they are hatched from eggs which have been stripped by hand from ripe females and fertilized with milt squeezed from males, pellet-fed to stock size [anything between 12 oz (340 g) and 10 lb (4·5 kg) plus] and then let free to be caught on artificial flies.

Some fisheries stock only once or twice a season, and in these waters, as the season progresses, it becomes increasingly harder to catch trout in quantity —or at least not until autumn when the catch-rate goes up as natural feed diminishes. Other waters are stocked weekly or monthly with batches of fish approximately equal in number to the total of fish caught during the preceding days or weeks, so ensuring a plentiful supply of catchable trout always being available for visitors.

Compared with coarse and sea fishing, which involve hunting only wild fish, modern-day trouting

(*above*) The Derbyshire Wye—domain of wild rainbow trout (*Peter Wheat*)

(*below*) Feeding time. Stock-pond rainbows swirl after the food-pellets thrown to them (*Peter Wheat*)

in 'put and take' waters is a very artificial branch of angling. Nevertheless, once it has been accepted that most, if not all of the fish caught, will have been stocked the same season at roughly the same size as when hooked, it will be found no less pleasurable than any other kind of fishing.

Contrary to the opinion sometimes voiced that 'stockies' are *always* easy to catch, it has been my experience that there are plenty of occasions every season when they prove extremely wily quarry, needing a fair degree of skill to entice to the fly. And what is more, even when they are simple to hook, such as on Opening Day, they still battle brilliantly enough to put any angler's ability to a full test. In that is the fascination of their catching.

Back in 1924, Lt.-Col. Creagh-Scott caught a natural-grown rainbow from Blagdon Reservoir, Avon, weighing 8 lb 8 oz (3·8 kg). This fish held the British record for 46 years, and then, in 1970, Brian Jones at last toppled it with an 8 lb 14 oz 12 drm (4 kg) stew-bred fish from a lake on the Packington Estate, West Midlands. Bigger and bigger stew-bred rainbows have been caught since, increasing the record many times, and already it is possible that fish weighing more than 30 lb (13·6 kg) will be caught from day-ticket fisheries before too long.

What the growth-limit for rainbows is, if indeed there is a limit, has still to be found out. But the rainbow weighing 37 lb (16·7 kg) from Lake Pend Oreille, Idaho, USA, in 1947, provides a clear idea of the potential of this species. Already a combination of selective breeding and heavy feeding has produced British rainbows exceeding the 30 lb (13·6 kg) mark. Despite the tremendous size of these fish, by my standard a 4 lb (1·8 kg) trout, rainbow or brown, is a big one, and one of 5 lb (2·2 kg) or over a red-letter specimen.

24

The author with a September-caught 5 lb 8 oz (2·4 kg) rainbow trout from Damerham Trout Lakes, Hampshire. It fell for a Whiskey Fly (*Peter Wheat*)

By nature, the true rainbow trout strain is a spring-spawner, but years of artificial breeding have led to the development of strains which spawn in the autumn/winter period in hatcheries. Mixed stocking of these different strains in angling waters has, unfortunately, led to spring-spawning rainbows attempting to breed at the same time as the trout season is getting under way, and autumn/winter spawning rainbows—reverting back to spring-spawning—being caught in a gravid state during every month of the season.

These ripe, out-of-condition fish, are no good for sport or to eat. It is hoped that eventually rainbow trout strains which spawn at the same time as brown trout and do not revert back, will be stocked universally to the total exclusion of spring-spawning strains.

Spawny rainbows are commonest at the start of the season—highly active, rapacious fish, which are incautious enough to grab at literally anything which moves near them. These dark-coloured fish are fat with eggs and milt, and the cocks (in their mating garb of purple gill-covers and flank stripes) defend territory by chasing after and tail-nipping other fish to warn them off.

'Blackies', as they are called, create two problems for the angler. First, they grab flies of every type, colour and size. Second, long areas of near-bank water will be occupied almost exclusively by them—the non-spawning 'silvers' having been driven off.

Avoiding the spawners, who usually stay close to the bank, is never easy. One answer is to hire a boat and search areas of the water further out. Another is to long-cast from the shore—putting the fly where it stands the best chance of contacting non-spawners.

The rainbow trout lives for four or five years, a comparatively short span compared with the 15 to 18 years of the brown trout. However, rainbows have the advantage of a faster growth-rate, and being also more easily and more cheaply reared to large size, they are preferred to browns as stock for 'put and take' fisheries.

In exactly the same way as the brown trout is a variety of the sea trout, so the rainbow trout is a variety of the steelhead trout of the USA. Like the sea trout, the steelhead trout is anadromous—that is, it spends part of its life in the sea (the Pacific Ocean). After three years in salt water, steelheads can weigh as much as 40 lb (18 kg) on their return to fresh water.

When rainbow strains of steelhead origin are stocked in rivers they migrate downstream and may, if they have an unrestricted passage, disappear completely.

Natural Food

Trout eat a wide variety of aquatic and terrestrial

organisms including plankton, insects, shellfish and small fish. Young trout subsist mainly on a diet of plankton and minute larvae, with larger items of food—nymphs, adult flies, shrimps, snails, earthworms, slugs and caterpillars, etc.—becoming more prominent on the menu as the fish increase in size.

Big trout eat lots of small fish such as minnows, sticklebacks, gudgeon, perch and immature trout. The biggest trout of all are confirmed fish-eaters perfectly capable of devouring other fish weighing 1 lb (0·4 kg) or more.

The variety of food featuring in the diet of trout (and all other fish) is governed by the forms of life present in the water. In this respect, the life-cycles of food-creatures living in and by the water, the individual seasons of their abundance, and the periods of the day when they are active, influence not only what is eaten but when it is eaten.

A large hatch of a particular insect, for example, may cause trout to become so preoccupied with eating it that they will completely ignore all other kinds of food, including insects which are closely similar. It is at such times that the angler, in order to overcome such single-mindedness, must angle with a pattern of artificial fly which as nearly as possible matches the size, shape and colour of the natural insect.

Some waters hold trout which exhibit a marked preference for types of food other than insect life. The famous gillaroo, for example, a massive-growing brown trout of Irish lakes, is such a confirmed eater of shellfish that its stomach lining has thickened to assist in dealing with this kind of diet.

Thames trout, long popular with anglers for their size and strength, are positively pike-like in their fondness for small fish. It is fairly uncommon to hook them on fly, and experienced anglers who trout-fish this river prefer such methods as trotting a small live fish beneath a float, spinning a dead fish mounted on a spinning flight, or searching the water with a spoon or plug, to fly fishing.

These methods are beyond the scope of this book. The concern here is solely fly fishing with fur and feather imitations of insects, small fish, and various other aquatic and semi-aquatic creatures.

2: TROUT DIET

The catching of trout on artificial fly is not an ultra-difficult task, but fly fishing in itself has become complex, and never more so than in the study of trout food and its mimicry on the hook.

Although such scholarship is totally absorbing, and a fascinating aspect of the sport to which many anglers give considerable attention, it is definitely not essential to hold a degree in aquatic entomology or own a box packed with hundreds of different patterns in order to get to grips with the catching of trout on artificial fly.

Absolutely nothing could be further from the truth. There are literally thousands of anglers taking trout in quantity every season who do not possess more than a rudimentary knowledge of what trout eat. And, though many of them may very well carry wallets filled with dozens of artificials, the chances are that they rely for the bulk of their success on just a handful of patterns in which they have great faith.

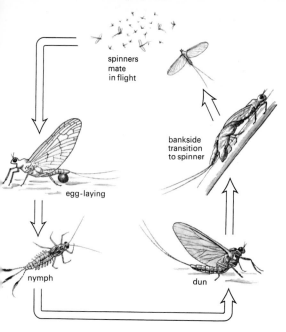

spinners
mate
in flight

bankside
transition
to spinner

egg-laying

nymph

dun

Stages in the life-cycle of ephemerid flies

As has been said many times: To fish with a fly you believe in, is nine-tenths of the way to persuading a fish to believe in it also.

Insects Imitated by the Angler

Upwinged Flies. Order EPHEMEROPTERA
The life-cycle of upwinged flies, of which there are over 40 species in Britain, commences with a clutch

of sticky eggs. The eggs of many species are dropped or laid by the female on to the surface of the water to sink below and find an anchorage as best they can. In other species the female crawls beneath the surface down the stems of plants to attach the eggs direct to underwater vegetation or the underside of stones.

From the eggs hatch the larvae or junior nymphs, which evolve through a series of moults into advanced senior nymphs—hump-backed creatures with three pairs of legs, wing-cases and three tail whisks. The nymphal stage usually lasts about one year, but extends to two years in some species.

When a nymph is 'ripe' it rises to the surface, and floating there, its outer skin, the nymphal shuck, splits at the shoulder to release the first winged form, the dun or sub-imago. Less commonly, in certain species, the dun emerges from the shuck under water, either floating to the surface or crawling ashore in a film of air. After resting for a short period on the surface or bank to stretch and dry its crumpled wings, the dun flutters heavily off and seeks a hiding-place in the bankside foliage to await the final metamorphosis into a breeding insect – the delicately-built spinner or imago. This transformation may take minutes or days depending on weather conditions and according to species.

After dancing together high in the air, the spinners mate and the females, either immediately or following a period of rest, dip down to the surface to shed their eggs. After doing so they fall exhausted on the water and float downstream, wings outstretched, as spent-spinners. The short life-span of the adults links the life-cycle of these flies, known as ephemerids.

Fish eat ephemerid flies at every stage of their

development: as maturing nymphs swimming and crawling along the bottom and through the weeds, as mature nymphs rising to the surface to hatch, as duns moving up through the water and drying on the surface, and as spinners ovipositing and expiring.

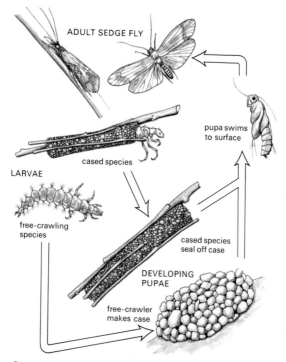

ADULT SEDGE FLY

pupa swims to surface

cased species

LARVAE

free-crawling species

cased species seal off case

DEVELOPING PUPAE

free-crawler makes case

Stages in the life-cycle of sedge flies

All these stages are imitated by the angler, and therefore it is already apparent that fly fishing has two main divisions: surface or dry-fly presentation and sub-surface or wet-fly presentation.

Sedge or Caddis Flies. Order TRICHOPTERA

The larvae of these flies are the caddis grubs which make such splendid natural baits for coarse fishing. Some are free-crawling species, but the majority are case-makers who construct cleverly camouflaged chambers from grains of sand, snail shell fragments and plant remains. Each sedge builds its own type of chamber, and many of the species can be identified by the unique structures they live in.

A point of passing interest is that case-making sedge grubs of fast water use heavier materials than those living in slow and still water, presumably to assist in anchoring themselves more firmly to the bottom in the swifter flow.

Sedge grubs, both free-crawlers and cased species, pupate and then hatch directly into fully mature flies, there being no sub-imago stage in their life-cycle.

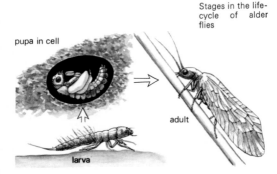

Stages in the life-cycle of alder flies

pupa in cell

adult

larva

32

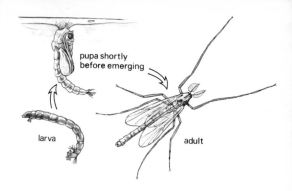

larva

pupa shortly
before emerging

adult

Stages in the life-cycle of chironomid flies

Alder Flies. Order MEGALOPTERA

The eggs of alder flies are laid in clusters on water-side plants. When the larvae hatch they fall to the ground and make their way to water where they live in the bottom silt for about two years. The larvae measure approximately 1 in (25 c·m) when fully grown, and at this stage they leave the water to pupate in bankside cells. They emerge as winged adults several weeks later.

Two-winged Flies. Order DIPTERA

This order includes: gnats, midges, mosquitoes, reed smuts, common house fly, bluebottle fly, crane fly, soldier fly, hover fly and drone fly.

Many of the DIPTERA species are imitated by the angler but, of them all, the most important from a fishing point of view are the chironomids. They number more than 400 separate species in Britain alone.

The chironomid life-cycle consists of egg, larva (including the bloodworm of coarse fishing),

33

pupa and winged adult. Bloodworm patterns have been devised and used with some success, but it is the pupae which are most frequently imitated by the angler. These active but legless little animals (the legs and wings of the adult insect can be seen through the transparent skin in the region of the thorax) rise steadily from the bottom and then 'hang' just under the surface for a short period prior to emerging as adult flies.

In lakes and reservoirs, chironomid pupae ascend in large numbers from the deepest areas of the water, and as they rise they attract feeding fish to follow them up to the surface. Still-water anglers who have taken the trouble to study the movements of chironomid pupae, and who have learned how to use the artificials in the right places, at the right times and in the right ways, catch a wealth of fine trout which probably would not be taken (at that time) by using any other type of fly or tactic.

Stone Flies. Order PLECOPTERA

These flies inhabit lakes, slow rivers, and the fast stony streams of north and west England, Scotland, Wales and parts of Ireland. Artificials of both the

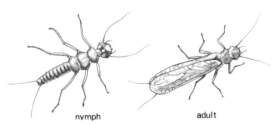

nymph   adult

A typical stone fly and nymph

34

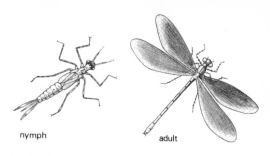

nymph

adult

A typical damselfly and nymph

nymphs (notably the nymphs of the Large Stone Fly known as 'creepers' on account of their poor swimming ability) and the adult flies are successful patterns for waters where these insects abound.

Other Insects Imitated by the Angler Include:

Dragonflies and Damselflies. Order ODONATA
During the months of June, July and August, trout are attracted to areas of thick weed to feed on ODONATA nymphs as they swim to the surface and crawl from the water to complete their transformation into adult insects. The artificial nymph should be worked closely along the margin of the weed at mid-depth and occasionally drawn up to the surface.

Bees, Wasps, Ants. Order HYMENOPTERA

Water Bugs. Order HEMIPTERA
Water crickets, water measurers, pond skaters, water scorpions, water boatmen and lesser water boatmen (Corixae).

Beetles. Order COLEOPTERA

35

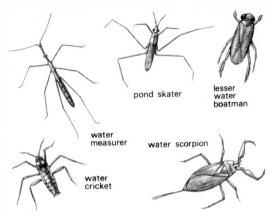

Water bugs

More Food

Water snails, water lice, water spiders, freshwater shrimps and small fish are all items in the diet of trout and coarse fish which are imitated by the angler.

It should be mentioned, in passing, that patterns tied to resemble non-flying creatures are also called flies. The terms 'lure' and 'streamer' describe patterns which are fish-like in colour and/or shape.

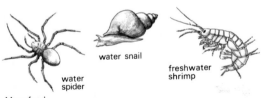

More food

A 3 lb (1·3 kg) trout and the contents of its stomach—
predominantly large water snails (*Fred J. Taylor*)

3: ARTIFICIAL FLIES

Artificial flies are fashioned from a wide range of
materials (including bird feathers, animal hair,
tinsel, silk, raffia, wool and chenille) mounted on
eyed hooks purposely designed for fly tying.

Fly-hooks with short and medium shanks are
suitable for dry flies, traditional wet flies and most

shanks		eyes		
short	long	down-turned	up-turned	straight

Hook features

nymphs. Long-shanked fly-hooks are used for lures, to take the longer, more fish-like bodies of these flies.

Keel-hooks, invented by American angler Dick Pobst, have crank-handle shanks which prevent patterns tied on them snagging weed and the bottom. As can be seen from the illustration, a keel-hook fly swims with its point uppermost, in line with the eye.

Traditional wet flies and lures tied on keel-hooks are excellent for 'bottom bumping' lakes and reservoirs to entice fish which are feeding deep. With an ordinary-hook fly this style of presentation is easily spoilt by the point catching up on snags and plant fragments.

Keel-hook fly

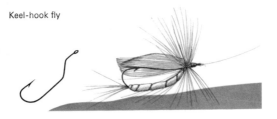

Fly Tying
Although shop-bought flies are reasonably priced considering the amount of time and skill which goes into their making, they are still far from cheap. The answer here is to tie your own flies at a fraction of the cost of ready-made flies.

This is not difficult. Simple patterns can soon be tied well enough to deceive trout, and with regular practice even the most intricate ones can be produced to a satisfactory standard.

A few tools, a book of instruction and a selection

Fly-tying kit

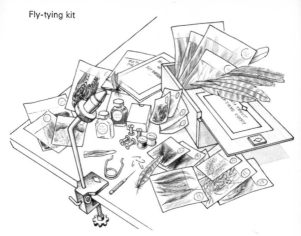

of materials are the basic requirements. But to make a start at fly tying, I suggest first obtaining the catalogue of E. Veniard Ltd, 138 Northwood Road, Thornton Heath, Surrey. This firm has long been a leading supplier of fly-tying items, and their comprehensive lists include every type of material and tool for the hobby, plus a first-rate series of beginners' kits, instructional books and other self-teaching aids.

It helps, of course, to be assisted by a knowledgeable friend, particularly at the very beginning when even the most straightforward operation will feel strange and awkward to carry out.

If you lack guidance of this kind, enquire locally if fly-tying classes are being held by angling clubs and other organizations in the area. A fly-tying course for complete novices, conducted by an expert, is an ideal foundation to the mastering of the techniques involved.

Multi-compart-
ment fly-box

Fly-Boxes and Fly-Wallets

For dry flies, which need to be protected from being
crushed in order to keep their springy hackles firm
and straight, I prefer a multi-compartment fly-box
which has each compartment fitted with an individual transparent lid. The flies can be held more
firmly by sticking magnetic strips along the bottoms
of the compartments, so preventing the contents
of a compartment being blown out by a sudden gust
when making a selection on a windy day.

I have long been of the opinion that the Bob
Church fly-wallet is the ideal container for nymphs,
wet flies and lures. This zip-up design consists of
four separated foam pads into which flies are stuck
in neat rows. Properly arranged, there is space for
well over 100 patterns of varying sizes.

Home-made fly-boxes are constructed by lining

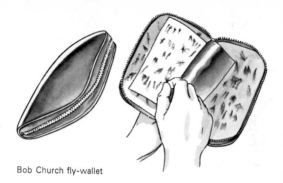

Bob Church fly-wallet

any flat box or tin with expanded polyethylene sheet.

A needle should be carried in the fly-box or fly-wallet for 'pricking out' the eyes of flies which have become clogged with varnish during the sealing off of the tying silk.

Selection

For hundreds of years generations of anglers have designed new flies in the hope that they would fool more fish than all the flies already invented. The

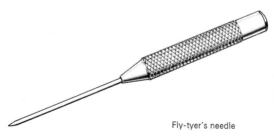

Fly-tyer's needle

Selecting the fly—a small but significant part of the sport's enjoyment (*Irish Tourist Board*)

results of this line of thinking are the thousands of artificials from which present-day anglers must make a choice.

However, no useful purpose would be served by giving a long and bewildering list of patterns. The ones mentioned on the following pages are representative selections to which beginners can add or subtract as their knowledge of different waters and the feed of the trout in them increases, and the fly-preferences of local experts become known.

4: ARTIFICIAL DRY FLIES

A typical dry-fly pattern is dressed with a ribbed body, two or three tail whisks (mainly if it is an ephemerid imitation) and a hackle made from stiff-fibred cock feather. It may also be fitted with split wings.

To perform as it should it must be capable of floating proud on the surface. And, therefore, it is essential that the materials of its construction repel water, and that the points of the hackle are springy enough to ride the surface 'skin'.

Some anglers choose to use thickly hackled dry flies for fishing fast water in places where conflictions of currents form a boisterous flow, but elsewhere sparsely hackled flies are better because of their more natural appearance.

Dry flies are treated with spray and dip-in floatants to keep them above water. Of the various brands currently available I consider Permaflote, developed by Richard Walker and Arnold Neave, as being superior to the rest. A fly dropped in this mixture, and then dried off completely, will float perfectly for a considerable length of time because Permaflote, unlike other floatants, does not wash off

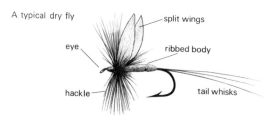

A typical dry fly

split wings

eye

ribbed body

hackle

tail whisks

easily once it has been 'fixed' by the drying process.

The selection of a pattern which matches either the hatching dun or the egg-laying spinner is clearly of importance, but it must also be borne in mind that an exact imitation which floats badly will be far less acceptable to trout than a well-tied fly of an indifferent pattern. Hence the fame of such generalized flies as the Lee Wulff series which, though they do not resemble particular insects, ride the water with a perfect balance.

It is vital that a dry fly 'looks right' in the water, as seen from below by a fish looking upwards. And in this respect it is worth mentioning the advantages of Dick Pobst's upside-down dry-fly hook, a version of the keel-hook principle.

Upside-down dry fly

Pobst hit on the idea in 1973 when he discovered that a slightly different weight distribution produced a hook which nearly always landed the fly in the water point up and bend down. A hook of this balance, tied as a dry fly, floats on the surface with its point clear of the water instead of dangling down sub-surface—a disadvantage of the ordinary hook long considered a key reason why trout are better able to discern the difference between a natural insect and its imitation no matter how well tied the artificial is.

Apart from not showing the hook to the fish, the

44

upside-down dry fly has other advantages over the ordinary dry fly:

Because the hook is not penetrating the surface it does not drag down the points of the hackle and waterlog the fly. The position of the hook-point also makes the fly as snag-proof as the original keel-hook. It can be dragged across weed and tweaked clear from the grass when a cast is misjudged for direction or distance with little risk of it becoming snagged. Furthermore, because the fly is completely above the water it is subject to slight changes of wind and current in exactly the same way as a natural fly is.

Another modern dry-fly hook which departs from traditional shape to improved presentation is the Mackenzie–Philps flybody hook. With an ordinary hook the body of the fly is tied along the

Mackenzie-Philps fly-body hook

shank, and this, as regular dry-fly fishermen well know, is far from being the most natural-looking style of fly imitation. The flybody hook is designed to improve on presentation by separating the body of the fly from the hook. The flybody hook is shankless, with the wire bent back along the top to form a U-shaped eye and give enough length of 'tail' to take the body of the fly independent of the hook. The point of the hook is situated well forward, hidden in the hackle.

Principal Upwinged Flies Include:

Olives   These common river and lake flies are

widely distributed throughout Britain and Ireland. Their main season lasts from early spring to late autumn, but they also appear in lesser numbers during the winter months. They include:

> Large Dark Olive   The earliest ephemerid species of the year, on the wing by March. *Patterns:* Blue Dun, Blue Quill, Rough Olive, Greenwell's Glory, Gold Ribbed Hare's Ear, Hackle Hare's Ear, Pheasant Tail, Lunn's Particular, Red Spinner, etc.

> Medium Olive   This fly, about the same size as the Large Dark Olive but lighter in colour, appears on the river from March onwards. *Patterns:* Olive Dun, Olive Quill, Greenwell's Glory, Gold Ribbed Hare's Ear, Hackle Hare's Ear, Red Spinner, Pheasant Tail, Flights Fancy, etc.

> Small Dark Olive   This species is the most olive-coloured member of the Pale Wateries. *Patterns:* imitations of the larger olives tied small.

> Blue Winged Olive   This river species is the only olive with three tail whisks. It is on the water from June onwards, mainly late evening. *Patterns:* Standard Blue Winged Olive, Lunn's Hackle Bluewing, Orange Quill, Sherry Spinner, Rusty Spinner, Pheasant Tail, Terry Thomas's B.W.O., etc.

> Lake and Pond Olives   *Patterns:* Red Spinner, Pheasant Tail, various standard olives.

Pale Wateries   A group of at least five different species. Principally, *Centroptilum luteolum, Centroptilum pennulatum, Procloeon rufulum, Baëtis bioculatus* and *Baëtis scambus* (Small Dark Olive). *Patterns:* Pale Watery Dun, Pale Watery Spinner, Little

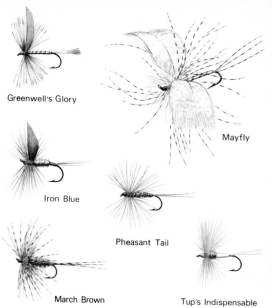

Greenwell's Glory

Mayfly

Iron Blue

Pheasant Tail

March Brown

Tup's Indispensable

Ephemerid dry flies (winged and unwinged patterns)

Marryat, Blue Quill, Ginger Quill, Little Amber Spinner, Lunn's Winged Yellow Boy, Flights Fancy, Tup's Indispensable, Pheasant Tail, Lunn's Particular, Gold Ribbed Hare's Ear, etc.

Iron Blue This small river-species is plentiful during late spring and autumn. It is often preferred by trout when hatching at the same time as olives or other larger flies. *Patterns:* Houghton Ruby, Halford's Jenny Spinner, Little Claret Spinner, Standard Iron Blue, etc.

March Brown   A large fly, abundant on some stony rivers (Welsh Usk, for example) between mid-March and the end of April. *Patterns:* Standard March Brown, Great Red Spinner, etc.

Mayflies   These big flies are localized in distribution to rivers in the midlands and south of England, and Irish limestone lakes and rivers. They are on the wing between late May and early June. Anglers call the sub-imago the Green Drake, the female imago the Grey Drake, and the male imago the Black Drake. The spent spinner is known as the Spent Gnat. *Patterns:* French Partridge, Grey Wulff, Lunn's Spent Gnat, etc.

Caënis (White Midge)   These five species are the smallest of the ephemerids. Their distribution extends to most parts of Britain and Ireland. *Caënis* duns cast their sub-imaginal skins within minutes of leaving the water, and the newly emerged spinners commence mating, followed by egg-laying, almost immediately. Fish feed mainly on the spinner stage.

When trout are preoccupied with *Caënis* (usually during early morning or late evening) it is sometimes possible to tempt them to accept a size 14, 16 or 18 midge pattern. This, however, is never easy fishing. It requires plenty of patience and very accurate casting—hence the fact that *Caënis* is commonly called the Angler's Curse.

A trout feeding on *Caënis* does so by gently sipping the insects from the surface in a series of small overlapping rises made to the same spot in the water. And therefore, to stand a reasonable chance of getting a response, it is essential to cast the artificial so that it travels down the current directly over this tiny patch of surface disturbance without alarming the fish. This, though, is easier said than done!

Rise pattern of a trout sipping *Caënis*

Silver Sedge   Cinnamon   Welshman's   Alder
                Sedge   Button

Sedge and alder dry flies

Sedge or Caddis Flies

More than 180 species of these moth-like insects
inhabit the rivers and lakes of Britain and Ireland.
They include: Cinnamon Sedges, Great Red Sedge,
Welshman's Button (a day-flyer), Silverhorn
Sedges, Grey Sedges (the Grey Flags of Irish
waters), Silver Sedge and the Grannom—a small
sedge of fast weedy streams which appears as early
as April in the south of England.

Sedge flies swarm freely on the surface at dusk in
warm weather, and then it is that trout rise to feast
on them with the wildest abandon until well into
full darkness.

Exact imitation of a particular sedge is rarely
necessary, and just two or three standard pale and
dark patterns in various sizes will cope adequately
with most situations arising.

Sedge artificials tied on keel-hooks are extremely
useful. I recommend them particularly for those
frustrating occasions when trout are tweaking
ordinary-hook sedge patterns on almost every cast
but not holding on firmly enough to set the hook.

Alder Flies

The adult alder fly is terrestrial rather than aquatic,
and arrives on the water by falling or being blown

off bankside herbage. May and June are its main season. One or two standard dry patterns are enough to cover the imitation of this insect.

Stone Flies

These flies, of which there are over 30 British species, inhabit lakes and both fast and slow rivers. Well-known species include: February Red: February and March, sluggish rivers. Willow Fly: autumn, slower rivers in midland and southern counties. Small Yellow Sally: May to July, fast upland streams. Early Brown: April and May, fast streams. Large Stone Fly: April to June, fast stony streams in northern and western England, Scotland, Wales and parts of Ireland.

Between late May and mid-June, a dry imitation of the Large Stone Fly (called the Mayfly in the north) often proves deadly on the trout streams of northern England. The female of this species is nearly 2 in (5 cm) long.

Black Gnats

During the warmer months of the year, the Black Gnat, *Bibio johannis*, is regularly to be seen on the water when the weather is muggy. Although it may blanket the whole of the river, it tends to produce local rather than general rises, and consequently, trout feeding on this insect—'smutting' as it is called—must be looked for carefully.

Trout taking these flies are rarely completely pre-occupied, and when they cannot be persuaded to respond to imitations such as J. W. Dunne's Black Gnat, Halford's Black Gnat or Peter Deane's Mating Black Gnat, they should be tried with a larger 'something different' pattern such as a small sedge. These 'shock tactics' produce excellent results at times.

Black Gnat   Daddy-long-legs   Coch-y-Bonddu

Popular dry flies

Reed smuts, midges and various other small *Diptera* species are all loosely described as black gnats by anglers. However, trout smutting these insects are usually totally preoccupied and consequently hard to tempt.

More Patterns
Hawthorn Fly (late April and May), Oak Fly (shady corners, June), House Fly, Bluebottle Fly, Cow-dung Fly, Flying Ant (August), Soldier Fly, Drone Fly, Daddy-long-legs (crane fly) and Coch-y-Bonddu (beetle).

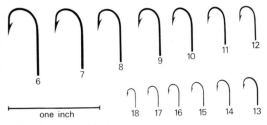

one inch   18 17 16 15 14 13

6   7   8   9   10   11   12

Hooks (Redditch scale)

Hooks

Fishing hooks are numbered according to their size. The higher the number the smaller the hook. Size 6 to size 18 hooks cater for most fly-tying needs. Dry flies are usually tied on size 10, 12, 14, 16 and 18 hooks.

5: ARTIFICIAL WET FLIES

Wet flies are winged and unwinged sub-surface patterns. There are three main groups: traditional wet flies; nymphs, pupae and larvae; lures. Fast-sink patterns are weighted with turns of fine wire. The hackles of hackled patterns are made from soft-fibred hen feather.

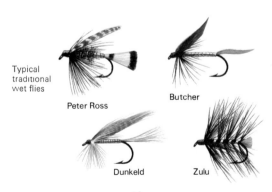

Typical traditional wet flies

Peter Ross

Butcher

Dunkeld

Zulu

Traditional Wet Flies

Wet flies, tied on medium-shank hooks, sizes 8 to 16, include artificials imitative of winged insects, and artificials—known as fancy or attractor flies—which, more or less, resemble fish-fry when jerked through the water.

Here is a selection of popular patterns: Butcher, Greenwell's Glory, Invicta, Zulu, Blae and Black, Red Tag, Wickham's Fancy, Dunkeld, Silver March Brown, Partridge and Orange, Teal, Blue and Silver, Mallard and Claret, Alexandre, Ginger Quill, Teal and Black, Peter Ross, Snipe and Purple, Tup's Indispensable, Grouse and Claret, Black and Peacock Spider, Olive Upright, Black Pennell and Cardinal.

Nymphs, Pupae and Larvae

This class consists of patterns tied to resemble the underwater stages of aquatic insects—ephemerid and Stone Fly nymphs, the larvae of alder flies, and the pupae of sedges, midges and chironomids, etc. Some of them are tied in imitation of individual insects (or insects which are superficially the same) such as, for example, the Hare's Ear Nymph and the Pheasant Tail Nymph, which imitate the nymphs of olive flies. Others, varying both in size and in colour, are semi-imitative generalized patterns of wider-ranging application.

Chironomid pupae patterns, known as buzzer nymphs or buzzer pupae, are tied on short-shanked and medium-shanked size 10, 12, 14 and 16 hooks. Green, brown, black, red, orange and yellow are useful colours.

Buzzers tied on size 8 hooks should also be carried in the fly-wallet for when there are millions of pupae on the move in the water. These are the times to try slightly larger, exaggerated buzzer patterns, which stand a better chance of being singled out from the naturals than do buzzer patterns of regular size. For this same purpose I also find Richard Walker's semi-imitative 'Chomper' series productive.

The big nymphs of mayflies, dragonflies and damselflies are tied on long-shanked hooks to allow for the extra length of body necessary in the imitation of these insects.

This group also includes nymph-like patterns of such creatures as shrimp, snail, water louse, tadpole, water spider, beetle and corixa (lesser water boatman). Two long-standing favourites of mine are the Leopard Nymph—a shrimp/corixa pattern, and the Long-Tail-Tit Nymph which looks rather like a tadpole.

Presentation is arguably more important than exact imitation when fishing a nymph, pupa or larva pattern. Many acknowledged experts in this

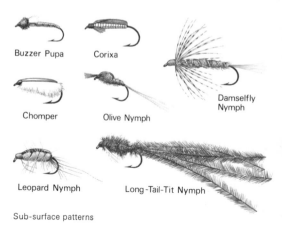

Buzzer Pupa

Corixa

Chomper

Olive Nymph

Damselfly Nymph

Leopard Nymph

Long-Tail-Tit Nymph

Sub-surface patterns

Don Stockton with a fine brown trout from Eglwys Nunydd Reservoir, Wales. It accepted a black lure worked slowly along the bottom through deep water (*Peter Rayment*)

field carry no more than two or three patterns for all their needs. And it is worth recalling that the late Major Oliver Kite, a truly outstanding fly-fisher and naturalist, caught many trout on a hook decorated with nothing more fancy than a few turns of copper wire along its shank.

Lures

The dividing line between traditional wet flies and lures is rather vague, to say the least. But, generally speaking, lures are larger and more fish-like than wet flies. And indeed, some patterns are instantly recognizable as imitations of sticklebacks, minnows, and the fry of perch, bream, rudd and roach.

Standard lures are dressed on size 6, 8 and 10 long-shanked single hooks. Double-hook tandem lures are employed for hunting reservoir trout and sea trout.

Patterns include: Appetiser, Black Chenille Lure, Standard Black Lure, Church Fry, Baby Doll, Missionary, Badger Matuka, Sweeney Todd, Muddler Minnow, Polystickle, Whiskey Fly, Orange Muddler, Jersey Herd, Poly-Butcher, White Muddler, Lime Green Lure, Sinfoils Fry, Hanningfield Lure, Ace of Spades, Minstrel, Scale Fry, Worm Fly, Squirrel and Orange, Texas Rose, Perch Fry, Grafham Norse and Mickey Finn.

Polystickle

Jersey Herd

Worm Fly Lure

Muddler Minnow

Sweeney Todd

Black Lure

Favourite lure patterns

6: TACKLE

Rods

Rods designed for fly fishing are manufactured from both fibre-glass tubing and split-cane. With the exception of certain specialized designs, they vary in length between 6 ft (1·8 m) and 10 ft (3 m).

Modern fly-fishing rods, balanced with correct lines, are versatile enough to meet the needs of many different circumstances. But it must be accepted that no single rod is capable of taking care of every set of circumstances likely to be encountered. For example, a longer, more powerful rod is needed to propel a lure far out across an exposed reservoir, than is required to present a tiny dry fly gently and accurately on a small stream. And so, before purchasing a rod, it must first be decided exactly what kind of fishing it will be used for: reservoirs and large lakes, small lakes, rivers, or small streams.

Rods for reservoirs and large lakes are between 8 ft 6 in (2·5 m) and 9 ft 6 in (2·9 m) long. A specific length much in favour these days is 9 ft 3 in (2·7 m). Such a rod in hollow fibre-glass weighs approximately 4 oz (113 g), and yet, despite its seeming frailty, it packs adequate power for long distance casting. It is not, of course, always necessary to put a fly 30–40 yd (27–36 m) out from the bank, but it is clearly advantageous to have a rod which will do this range *if needed*. Trout in hard-fished, day-ticket reservoirs, are more likely to be gathered well away from the edge than close in during the greater part of the day, often coming no nearer to the bank than 30 yd (27 m) or there-abouts.

It is rather easier to cast long distance with a split-cane reservoir rod, but militating against this slight advantage is the sheer weight of a cane rod—which weakens the wrist and arm when casting con-tinuously and makes control of the tackle increas-ingly more difficult. This is a major reason why most reservoir anglers choose lightweight fibre-glass rods of no greater length than 9 ft 6 in (2·9 m).

However, one highly skilled school of still-water troutmen—the Northampton school—also include in their kit extra-powerful rods of 10 ft (3 m). A rod of this class in fibre-glass weighs 7½ oz (212 g)—heavy compared with the normal run of fibre-glass reservoir rods, but nothing like so weighty as a split-cane model of similar specifications.

Large reservoirs are barren places subject to strong winds—conditions easy enough to master when fishing with the wind or along a becalmed sheltered corner, but daunting, to say the least, when casting out from an exposed shore receiving the full force of the blow.

This is where the Northampton-style 10-footer (3 m) comes into its own. It is a perfect weapon for searching rough water from the bank as it has the essential backbone to punch a heavy line out through the wind. Also, it is a less tiring rod to use for distance casting, as less energy is expended in false casting. Just two or three false casts are usually all the seasoned angler requires to make a 30–40 yd (27–36 m) cast with a rod of this calibre.

Rods for small lakes are less powerful than those for use on reservoirs. A rod of 8–9 ft (2·4–2·7 m), in either fibre-glass or split-cane, is suitable for these waters.

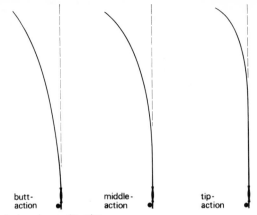

| butt-action | middle-action | tip-action |

Rods under equal tension

River rods are also of 8–9 ft (2·4–2·7 m) length. A fibre-glass model makes a handy all-rounder for fishing dry and wet fly, but for presenting a dry fly, or a wet fly upstream, with *absolute* accuracy, there can be no doubting that a well-made split-cane rod is by far the wisest choice.

Small streams, providing they are not too over-grown, can be fished with river-length rods, but shorter rods—between 6 ft 6 in (1·9 m) and 7 ft 6 in (2·2 m)—are splendid from a purely sporting point of view for the increased 'action' they offer, even against fish of 'tiddler' size.

The following points should be considered when purchasing a fly-fishing rod:

The action of a fly rod—indicated by the shape

of its bend when under tension—is according to the taper along its length. The three principal actions are termed tip-action, middle-action and butt-action.

Tip-actioned rods flex fast and are particularly suitable for long casting matched with heavy lines.

Middle-actioned and butt-actioned rods flex more slowly, and are ideal for casts of average length using lighter lines. They present the fly with greater finesse than do tip-actioned rods.

Extreme actions—tip or butt—are not advisable for beginners. It is far better to start off with a rod of less pronounced action, such as a middle-to-tip actioned fibre-glass rod for long-distance casting, or a middle-to-butt actioned rod, in either fibre-glass or split-cane, for lesser distances, and to graduate to a tip-actioned or butt-actioned rod when casting ability has been improved—if indeed a change of

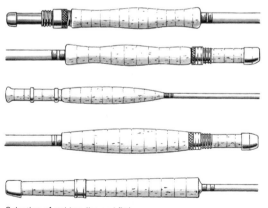

Selection of rod handles and fittings

rod action is then considered desirable, bearing in mind that the action of a rod must suit an individual's physique as much as anything else. There is no sense in buying a fast-actioned rod if it is going to be too powerful to flex properly over a period of several hours continuous casting.

The fly-rod handle is short, covered with cork, and shaped to form a comfortable hand-grip when held in the casting position.

The attachment for the reel, situated at the bottom of the handle, must hold the reel's saddle firmly, with no wobble. Screw-grip connection is the most reliable type, but lightweight sliding fittings are better for 'midge' rods, where parts of an ounce can make a big difference to the action of the cast and the 'feel' of the tackle.

Quality rod rings are made from very hard lightweight metals, finished ultra-smooth to reduce friction. Some butt and tip rings are lined with a special anti-friction material such as 'Sintox', 'Agatine', 'Aqualite' or 'Hardloy'.

It is most important that the diameter of the tip ring is large enough not to create excessive friction as the line runs through it. Friction reduces casting distance, and at the same time increases wear on the skin of the fly line. A too small tip ring also prevents the knots joining the leader to the fly line and the fly line to the backing passing through without catching up.

Intermediate rings are of two types: 'full-open bridge' and 'snake'. Snake rings are marginally better than bridge rings because they bend with the rod and do not interfere with its action. Furthermore, they are lighter than bridge rings, and therefore superior as fittings for lightweight rods.

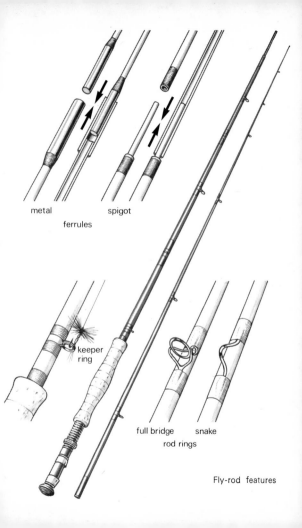

metal

spigot

ferrules

keeper ring

full bridge   snake

rod rings

Fly-rod features

Occasionally, a rod ring gets chipped or becomes rough-edged, and in such a state can easily rip a fly line and ruin it beyond repair. To prevent this happening, all rings should be checked for damage at the end of each day's fishing, and any found defective—even slightly so—replaced without delay.

Some rods have a tiny ring or eye whipped on just above the handle. This is the 'keeper ring', and its purpose is to hold the fly when the rod is not in use. If no keeper ring is fitted, the fly should be hooked through the butt ring—never into the cork of the handle.

Ferrules join the sections of a fly rod together. The metal type consists of a male part on the top joint and a female part on the bottom joint. Both parts should be treated with a spray lubricant prior to fitting the sections together, to prevent them gripping so tightly that they cannot be pulled apart again.

The modern spigot ferrule (fibre-glass rods only) consists of a fibre-glass 'plug' fixed in the top end of the bottom joint which jams firmly into the bottom end of the top joint. This simple design is always first choice for fibre-glass rods these days.

To keep a split-cane rod in good condition it should be wiped down after use and hung up in a loosely-tied bag in a dry atmosphere away from any form of direct heat. *Never* stow a split-cane rod away while it is still wet, or dampness will be sure to penetrate (particularly under the cork) and warp the wood. Attempting to dry a rod in front of a fire will also warp the wood. Scratches and chips should be filled with a coat or two of varnish.

Fibre-glass rods are not so easily damaged through lack of attention, but to be on the safe side I always

Casting with a high-gloss rod can scare fish

take just as much care with 'glass' rods as I do with split-cane rods.

Commercially produced rods are rarely finished with anything other than coats of high-gloss varnish—nice to look at it's true, but a positive disadvantage when it comes to practical fishing. A high-gloss rod flexed back and forth through the air on a bright day will catch the sun again and again, and give off warning flashes to any fish which might be cruising through the water close by.

This problem is solved by dulling the high-gloss varnish with an extra coat of matt varnish. Treated in this way, a rod may not look so attractive as when bought, but at least it will no longer send fish bolting for cover!

Do-it-yourself rod kits are sold by firms specializing in this branch of the tackle trade. Many excellent fly-fishing sets are available, including quite a few which have the more difficult tasks already completed, and which can be built to a very high standard with just a few simple tools plus the instructions provided.

The significant thing about DIY rod making is that a kit costs a surprisingly moderate amount compared with the price of the finished article.

There is little risk of failure. In fact, several rods I made as a boy, with no adult at my elbow, are still doing stalwart service to this very day.

Graphite, also called carbon-fibre, is a fairly new rod material with tremendous potential for fly-fishing needs. It was invented during the mid-sixties at the Royal Aircraft Establishment, Farnborough in Hampshire, and since then it has been developed for various purposes including fly-rod construction, mainly in America and Japan.

Most graphite rods have 'all-through' (middle and middle-to-butt) actions. Strong, versatile and sensitive, they flex crisply, work well for accuracy and distance, and are slimmer and lighter than other rods—about 25% lighter than equivalents in fibre-glass and about 40% lighter than those in cane.

Continuous casting is a strain on the muscles—even the trained muscles of experts—and the heavier and thicker the rod is, the more of an effort it becomes to maintain carefully measured casts and to punch a fly a long way out through the teeth of a raging wind.

With a slim-built graphite rod, almost the whole of the casting effort is put where it matters most—into working the line, rather than into working the rod, backwards and forwards.

Graphite rods are available in Britain, but at

current prices they are very much in the luxury class and well beyond the pocket of the average man.

Should ways be found to lower the cost of graphite, however, I am convinced that fly rods in this material will become every bit as popular as fibreglass and split-cane rods are now.

Reels

The purpose of the reel is to hold the fly line and a sufficient length of backing line. It should never be larger—therefore heavier—than is required to provide the capacity for this purpose.

Single-action reels are the most popular. A reel of this type has a caged drum and either an enclosed

Single-action reel. Top right: exposed-flange reel. Bottom right: enclosed-flange reel

or exposed flange. Small fish can be handled quite easily with an enclosed-flange reel, but for big fish it is far more reliable to use a reel which has an exposed flange—so that sensitive pressure can be exercised with the fingertips against the edge of the flange when a powerful specimen charges off at speed.

Some single-action reels are fitted with adjustable drag systems which can be regulated to increase or decrease the resistance against line being taken from the drum. This refinement is helpful, but by no means an essential feature of a good reel.

Multiplying reels are geared so that each turn of the handle rotates the drum more than once and gives a very fast recovery of the line. This is a major advantage when a fish hooked on a long line turns and swims towards the bank. The slackening of the line when this happens greatly increases the risk of the hook falling out if it has not taken a firm hold in the lip of the fish, and so it is always vital to tighten up this slack as quickly as possible.

However, multiplying reels are more expensive to buy than single-action reels. They are also designed with more complex mechanisms, which in-

Left: multiplying reel. Right: automatic reel

crease their weight slightly. Both enclosed—flange and exposed—flange models are available. Some feature adjustable drag systems.

Automatic reels have clockwork mechanisms which wind up each time line is stripped from the drum. A slipping clutch arrangement prevents over-winding.

This type of reel has no handle, and line is retrieved by depressing a rewind lever with the little finger of the hand holding the rod. This lever is operated the whole time a fish is being played.

I freely admit that I dislike automatic reels. In my view, they are too heavy and do not provide the same sensitive control over big fish which exposed-flange single-action reels offer. Definitely not reels for beginners.

Fly reels are fitted with quick-release drums to allow changes of line to be made with a minimum of delay. At least two drums are required for fishing small lakes and rivers, and three or four for reservoirs.

Reels should be cleaned regularly and retained in padded zip-up bags to protect them from grit, knocks and scratches.

Padded reel protector with zip

Lines

A typical modern fly line consists of a braided nylon 'core' covered by a plastic 'skin'. Apart from wiping off scum and mud, either with a cleaning agent *recommended by the manufacturer* or, better still, with a cloth soaked in soapy (not detergent) water, it requires no maintenance. It can, for example, be left on the reel soaking wet without fear of it degenerating—as would certainly happen with a line of the old-fashioned silk kind, still favoured in some circles.

Nevertheless, care must be taken not to spoil the outer coat of a plastic line by bruising or pinching it, or bringing it into contact with oil, petrol, grease, detergent, fly and leader floatants, or line cleaners that are not recommended by the manufacturer.

Fly lines are completely different from those used in other branches of angling. They are thicker than ordinary fishing lines, and they taper along their lengths according to the shape of their profile.

The three basic profiles are double-taper, forward-taper and long-belly taper. Average length: 30 yd (27 m).

A double-taper line has a parallel belly in its middle section and tapers equally at each end. When the outside end becomes badly worn the line is reversed on the drum to extend its life.

A double-taper line is thick, heavy, and poor for long-distance casting. It will, however, cast a fly accurately and put it down on the surface softly, and for these reasons is ideal when it comes to presenting a dry fly or nymph to an individual fish.

A forward-taper line, also known as a weight-forward or torpedo line, tapers at one end only.

Directly behind the 10 ft (3 m) taper of a typical forward-taper line, there is a 20 ft (6 m) belly backed by a long thin shooting line spliced in. This profile makes a good line for long-distance casting, and for casting into a wind.

The forward end of a forward-taper line—the section aerialized to bring shooting line through the rings—varies from approximately 30 ft (9 m) to approximately 40 ft (12 m), according to line size and the specifications of different manufacturers.

A long-belly line incorporates many of the advantages of both double-taper and forward-taper lines.

A double-taper line is first-class for short distances. It casts smoothly, delivers the fly naturally and, because of its long parallel body, possesses good flexibility of lift. Its one big disadvantage is that it does not shoot line, and therefore, to reach any great distance with a double-taper, there is need for considerable false casting—tiring on the arm, and often far too slow a delivery to cover a fish moving by.

A forward-taper line is designed to shoot line—so reducing the need for excessive false casting, and making long casts relatively easy to perform. But, while trout which are far out can be reached with a minimum of delay, it is not so easy to present the fly softly. Moreover, it is necessary to retrieve a very large part of a forward-taper line before 'lifting out' for the next cast.

Most casts are, of course, retrieved to as close as possible. But occasions do occur when a fish will suddenly commence to rise near by at a moment when a retrieve is only partly completed, and then it is difficult to resist the temptation to lift out into a back cast, with shooting line still beyond the rod tip, in an effort to cover the rising fish quickly. The usual result from such an attempt is the line collapsing in one almighty heap around the ears!

A long-belly line, as its name indicates, has an extended belly-length—varying, tip to end of belly, between 41 ft (12 m) and 55 ft (16 m) according to line size—which gives wider flexibility of lift-length than is possible from a conventional forward-taper profile.

The long-belly profile performs virtually as a double-taper for casting, with the thinner section coming into play only when shooting for distance. However, to use a long-belly line in exactly the same way as a normal forward-taper—particularly in aerializing the taper *completely* beyond the rod tip—requires a very high degree of casting proficiency.

Double-taper, forward-taper and long-belly taper lines are known as 'full' fly lines. The other main type is known as the shooting-head.

Shooting-heads are favoured by a few anglers for fishing rivers and small lakes, but their main advantage is for long distance casting across reservoirs and similar big waters.

A shooting-head is really nothing more than one end of a double-taper line attached to shooting line or monofilament backing. Standard shooting-head length is 30 ft (9 m), but shooting-heads both longer and shorter are also used according to individual needs.

An alternative to buying a ready-made shooting-head is to purchase a double-taper line and cut a shooting-head from each end—snipping and adjusting their lengths to suit personal requirements. I suggest that newcomers to fly fishing do not attempt this task without the guidance of an associate who has had plenty of shooting-head experience. Mistakes are costly!

double-taper

forward-taper

shooting-head

Fly-line profiles

A special casting technique enables a shooting-head to be propelled a tremendous distance—over 40 yd (36 m) in the hands of a really capable angler.

Fly lines further divide into floaters, sinkers and wet-tips.

Floaters are double-taper, forward-taper, long-belly taper and shooting-head lines with a specific gravity lighter than that of water. They are used to present dry flies and sub-surface patterns in shallow water and the upper levels of deep water. I prefer a white or blue-white floater to that of any other colour. Lying on the surface, such a line blends with the lighter background of the sky and is therefore less easily identified by the fish.

Sinkers are double-taper, forward-taper and shooting-head lines with a specific gravity heavier than that of water. Some types sink fast, others more slowly. They are used to present sub-surface patterns at every depth. Brown and green are the two colours I like best for sinkers. Both of them camouflage nicely with underwater terrain.

Wet-tips are double-taper, forward-taper and long-belly taper floaters with short lengths [5 yd (4·5 m) or less] of sinking line spliced into their casting ends. A part-sinking profile prevents a wet fly lifting and skidding the surface when fishing down a stretch of

73

fast water, and is also a boon for searching intermediate depths of reservoirs and lakes when it is suspected that fish are feeding on nymphs and pupae ascending to the surface. A nymph or pupa artificial worked 'on the drop' produces excellent sport at times, and a wet-tip line achieves this style of presentation far better than any other profile. Surface movement, created by a prevailing wind, helps activate the fly or flies by bowing and drifting the floating part of the line.

For rivers and small lakes, I use double-taper, forward-taper and long-belly taper floating lines. I switch over to sinkers and wet-tips only when fishing swift-flowing rivers, small lakes of exceptional depth, and small lakes generally when low water temperatures have sent the fish deep and unresponsive to any ploy other than a fly retrieved slowly along the bottom past their noses.

For reservoirs, my choice is forward-taper floating

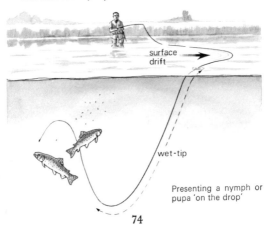

surface drift

wet-tip

Presenting a nymph or pupa 'on the drop'

74

and wet-tip lines when surface fishing and searching shallows and the upper levels of deep water, and slow-sink and fast-sink shooting-heads for distance casting and investigating the lower levels of deep water.

Other lines I carry include a floating shooting-head for near-surface lure fishing at long range, and a home-made, ultra-fast sinking, *level* diameter shooting-head [constructed from 20 ft (6 m) of lead-cored trolling line], for bottom-bumping the deepest of reservoir 'holes' from a boat.

Building up a set of fly lines for reservoir fishing is, without doubt, an expensive undertaking, and is best spread out over several seasons. Initially, it is possible to get by with just two lines—a forward-taper floater and a fast-sink shooting head.

Looked after correctly, a quality fly line will last a minimum of three or four seasons.

The AFTM scale is a system devised by the American committee of the Association of Fishing Tackle Manufacturers which classifies fly lines according to the weight of the first 30 ft (9 m) (excluding the level tip-length).

Lines are numbered from 1 to 12—the higher the number the heavier the line. As a broad guide, lines numbered 7, 8, 9 and 10 match rods for reservoirs and large lakes and big-river sea trout fishing. Small-lake rods match lines numbered 5, 6 and 7. And rods for rivers and small streams match lines numbered 4, 5, 6, and 7.

Every line and rod is marked with an AFTM number. Casters of average ability simply have to pair up the number on the line packaging with the number on the rod (just above the handle) to obtain a correctly balanced outfit—a line heavy enough when cast to work the 'spring' of the rod, but not so heavy that it overloads it.

Having said that, it must be emphasized that the AFTM scale is worked out according to the weight of the first 30 ft (9 m) of line *aerialized beyond the rod tip*.

It follows, therefore, that beginners who cannot yet aerialize very much line will not have enough *line weight* moving through the air to work the rod fully. This also applies when fishing a small stream or a tiny pool where casting range is reduced to 10–20 ft (3–6 m), or casting into a strong wind. This difficulty is countered by selecting an AFTM line marked *one size heavier* than the AFTM number of the rod.

An experienced caster, on the other hand, capable of aerializing far more line than average, selects, when required, a line *one size lighter* than that indicated for the rod to create a better working balance, and so prevent the rod being strained or broken against more weight of line than it was designed to flex.

As well as the AFTM number, the packaging of a line also includes a letter code on either side of the number which provides a full description of its function. Here are two examples:

DT–6–F designates the line as a number 6, Double-Taper, Floating line.

ST–9–S designates the line as a number 9, Shooting-Taper (Shooting-Head), Sinking line.

Letters and their meanings are as follows:

DT = Double-Taper. WF = Weight-Forward (Forward-Taper).

ST = Shooting-Taper (Shooting-Head). F = Floating line.

S = Sinking line. F/S = Floater/Sinker (Wet-Tip).

L = Level line.

VFS = Very Fast Sinker.

Nearly every line sold in Britain includes a stick-tab printed with its line code. The stick-tab is attached to the reel drum containing the line as an easy means of reference.

Never leave a line lying around exposed to hot sunlight. Out of season, remove all lines from their drums and stow them, loosely coiled, away from light and heat.

Backing line is essential because a full 30 yd (27 m) fly line is not long enough to eliminate the risk of a big fish emptying the drum completely. Braided terylene or monofilament of 15–20 lb (7–9 kg) test is used for this purpose—attached firmly to the reel drum by means of the following knot:

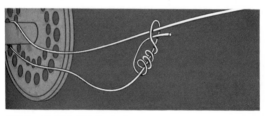

Attachment of backing line to drum

The combined length of the backing line and the fly line should almost fill the drum in order to provide the fastest rate of retrieval. If the drum is underfilled, less line will be recovered for each turn of the handle. I hasten to add though that it is even more important not to overfill the drum, as this could result in a build-up of line on one side of the drum jamming tight against the cage of the reel.

Only a small amount of backing line is required for rivers, but for lakes, particularly those holding trophy-size fish, a full fly line should be supported by at least 50 yd (22·6 m) and a shooting-head by no less than 100 yd (91 m).

Monofilament of 20–26 lb (9–11 kg) test makes ideal shooting-backing for a shooting-head outfit, and the best, in my opinion, is Tapeworm, devised by Don Neish. This type of monofilament is flat and less prone to tangling than ordinary round monofilament. It also has a large surface area which helps it to remain afloat when greased.

The needle knot is extremely reliable for joining monofilament backing line to a shooting-head or a full fly line.

The needle knot

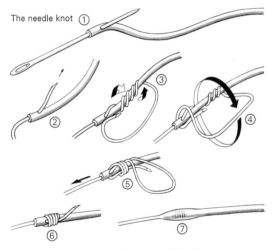

1 Make hole in fly line with needle.   **2** Push pointed monofilament through and out of the side.   **3** Take turns of monofilament round line.   **4** Take turns in the opposite direction.   **5** Pull on monofilament to tighten turns.
6 Trim end of monofilament.   **7** Varnish to complete.

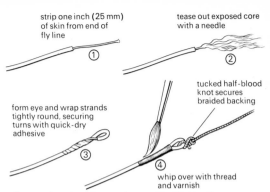

Construction of eye for attachment of braided backing to a full fly line

Before commencing to cast with a shooting-head outfit, it is a good idea to run the monofilament out along the bank and give it a firm stretch to limpen it up.

Monofilament needs to be checked regularly for strength as it has a tendency to weaken unexpectedly. Backing line should be replaced as soon as it becomes suspect—and always at the start of a new season. Never take chances with last year's backing line. If it parts during a forward cast, or when playing a hefty fish, the expensive fly line will almost certainly be lost.

Leaders

The leader, or cast, is the length of monofilament which links the end of the fly line to the fly. Usually it is 9 ft (2·7 m) in length, but it can be shorter for a short rod or longer—to improve presentation—

when attempting to deceive shy fish or to work a fly deep on a floating line.

A tapered leader reduces down from a thick butt to a thin point, and it is the anatomy of this reduction which decides between the leader being a good or bad one. Butt thickness should equal, as far as that is possible, the thickness of the fly line tip. The diameter of the point, generally speaking, varies according to the size of the fly to be fished.

There are two basic types of leader: knotless and knotted. The latter type, constructed by joining pieces of monofilament of different lengths and thicknesses, is cheaper to make than to buy. It is, however, essential to use correct formulae in order to produce really good knotted leaders which will present the fly accurately and crisply. Information of this kind, based on research by French expert Charles Ritz, is available in instructional kits from Nether Wallop Mill. (See page 92.)

Blood knot

The four-turn blood knot and the four-turn water knot are both used to connect the different sections of knotted leaders. The water knot is rated to be the stronger of the two, but personally I have never found cause to doubt the reliability of the easier-to-tie blood knot, which is the one I prefer. Monofilament knots should be tied with great care and always moistened before being pulled tight.

A leader is greased to make it float, and pulled through a ball of fuller's earth mixed with washing-up liquid to make it sink. If the ball is kept in an

The shadow from a floating leader may scare fish

airtight container it will remain pliable for several years at least.

Quick-sink type leaders, which break the surface film the instant they touch water, are useful not only for sub-surface fishing but also to present a dry fly sunken-leader style. This is always a technique worth trying when it is suspected that the shadow of a floating leader is scaring the fish.

As already mentioned, the thickness of the leader point relates to the size of the fly. A big fly needs a stiff point to force it to turn over at the end of the cast, and also to enable the thicker-wired hook to be struck home hard without fear of breaking the

A stiff leader point forces a big fly to turn over

leader. A small fly, on the other hand, both looks and behaves less naturally when tied on a thick point.

However, a further consideration which must be taken into account when selecting point thickness is the 'possible' size of the fish likely to be caught. Many lakes are now stocked with trout of truly massive proportions, and where such lunkers are present in the water it is plainly inviting trouble to angle a tiny fly on a fine leader point. Every season big fish are lost by anglers who use 'sporty', understrength gear, and frankly there is nothing at all commendable about these happenings, which can so easily be avoided.

The loss of a lunker trout always annoys me. I would really rather not have hooked the fish in the first place. And hence my policy when fishing a big-trout water to start off the day by using the largest fly I believe will tempt fish, tied on a stout leader. Later on, should I decide to scale down to a smaller fly, I still continue using a thick point in the firm conviction that though the fly will not behave as well as it would on a thin point, at least if it is taken by a big fish there is a better than average chance of winning the fight and netting the fish— which after all is the object of casting out the fly in the first place.

In passing, it is worth noting that many big-trout hunters are now using small flies tied on large hooks. For example, Richard Walker fished a Partridge and Orange tied short on a size 6 hook to take an 18 lb 4 oz (8·2 kg) rainbow trout from the Avington Fishery in Hampshire, during April 1976. Conventionally, the length of the dressing suited a size 12 hook.

Low diameter/high breaking strain monofilament is best for making leaders. Leaders tapering to 2, 3, 4, 5 and 6 lb (2·7 kg) at point are sufficient for most

Well-known angler Richard Walker with a magnificent 18 lb 4 oz (8·2 kg) rainbow trout from Avington Fishery, Hampshire. At time of capture the largest rod-caught rainbow from British waters (*Angling Times*)

circumstances, while points of 7, 8, 9 and 10 lb (4·5 kg) test are more suitable for waters containing trout of double-figure calibre. The life of a leader can be extended by renewing its point-length regularly.

Some leaders have droppers attached. These are

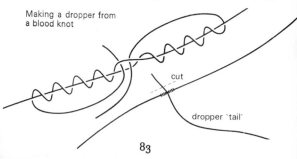

Making a dropper from a blood knot

cut

dropper 'tail'

short 'tails' formed from knot ends, and their purpose is to carry additional flies to the one on the point. For certain kinds of fishing a team of two or three evenly spaced flies is an advantage, but not always.

Too often things can go wrong when using a multi-fly rig. Tangles increase for a start. And when a lively fish is hooked there is always a risk that 'empty' flies will catch on weed and snags, the landing net mesh, or even hook additional fish.

I once lost a very large brown trout, which I had connected on the point fly of a two-fly team, because a much smaller trout, attracted by the cavortings of its fellow, homed in and grabbed the dropper fly so forcefully that the straining leader broke above both fish!

Only occasionally do I now use more than one fly at a time, and never when angling a water where fish run big and need extensive playing to tire them.

A three-fly team consists of a point or tail fly, a first dropper fly, and a top dropper or bob fly.

Leaders can conveniently be kept in individual grip-edged plastic bags, marked according to point strength/diameter and carried in a compartmented leader wallet. A new leader which remains 'coily' after it has been opened out, can be straightened by drawing it through a piece of rubber such as a square of old inner tube.

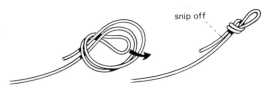

Forming an eye at the end of the tail

All my fly lines have 18 in (45 cm) 'tails' of 20–25 lb (9–11 kg) monofilament needle-knotted to their tips. A leader is attached to a tail by a four-turn blood knot, or by half-blooding it to a tiny eye at the end of the tail. Alternatively, a cast connector can be used to join leader and fly line *direct*. The illustration explains how this simple but efficient device works. A cast connector can also be used to attach the backing line to a full fly line.

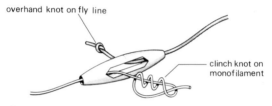

overhand knot on fly line

clinch knot on monofilament

Cast connector

Although correctly tapered leaders are important tackle in the fly-fisher's bag, they are not essential for all types of fishing. For example, Bob Church, one of Britain's leading exponents of reservoir trouting, prefers 9 or 15 ft (2·7 or 4·5 m) of level monofilament straight from the spool for fishing single lures—selecting a breaking strain according to the size of trout he expects to catch. For hunting reservoir trout with a dry fly—a sedge pattern—he chooses 9 or 12 ft (2·7 or 3·6 m) of 6 lb (2·7 kg) test.

In the final analysis, each angler must decide for himself whether a carefully tapered leader is needed for the fishing he is engaged in, or whether a level length of monofilament will be sufficient.

Monofilament does not rot, and for this reason is

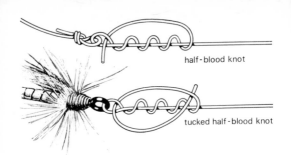

half-blood knot

tucked half-blood knot

an absolute menace to wildlife. *Waste pieces should always be taken home and burnt, never thrown away along the bank.*

The tucked half-blood knot is reliable for attachment of the fly to the leader. The leader-end can be more easily threaded through the fly's eye by holding the fly up against the light background of the sky.

Further tackle

The priest is a truncheon-like tool used for administering the 'last rites' to trout. A fish can, of course, be killed by knocking its head against a hard surface, or by bending its head back far enough to break its neck. But these are messy, unsatisfactory

Priest

methods, compared with the priest.

To dispatch a trout speedily with a priest, the fish should be held against the ground on its belly and thumped several times over the head, above the eyes and gill-covers, with the leaded end of the tool.

Polaroid sunglasses cut out surface glare almost completely on bright days. Wearing a pair makes it possible to see a dry fly more easily, the twitch of the line when a nymph pattern is taken, or to look *into* the water to spot where fish are lying. Also, when a takeable fish has been 'marked down', the angle and length of the cast can be judged to a nicety, and the reaction of the fish to the fly observed clearly. This is always an exciting thing to experience, but never more so than when a lunker trout is watched at close quarters as it opens its mouth to gulp in the fly.

Split-shot (tiny grooved lead pellets) are used to sink buoyant patterns deep. For this purpose a single shot is pinched on the cast directly above the fly. The 'plop' of a shotted fly entering the water will sometimes entice a trout to rush in and grab the fly without hesitation.

A waterproof bag is needed to hold spare tackle, clothing and refreshment. Plenty of designs are available, and the more expensive ones are fitted

Split-shot

Fly-fisher's bag

with several compartments including a washable section for *temporary* retention of the catch. An ex-service back-pack, treated with a waterproofing agent, makes a suitable alternative to a specialized tackle carrier.

Sundries include a pair of sharp, tightly-bladed scissors for clipping monofilament, and a carborundum stone for honing the points of blunted hooks.

A further item is a rod-keeper. Reservoir anglers often rig two rods ready for an immediate change of method—for example, one rod with a shooting-

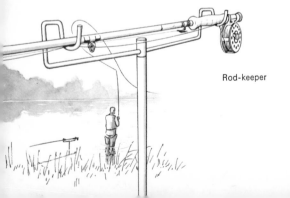

Rod-keeper

head and lure, and the other with a wet-tip and nymph. Rather than leave the spare rod lying on the bank where it might get trodden on by a passing angler, it is placed in a rod-keeper.

Moreover, when wading, a rod-keeper helps to avoid the fish-scaring disturbance of the water which is caused by paddling in and out to change rods. For this purpose the rod-keeper and spare rod are positioned slightly behind the angler on his non-casting side with the rod pointing towards the bank.

Clothing

A really good fishing jacket is an expensive item to buy, but properly cared for it will last a great many years, and as such is a justified investment for the regular angler. A top-quality waterproof design has a detachable lining and hood, stormproof cuffs and collar, and plenty of button-over pockets. Ideally, it should be three-quarter length to protect the rear when sitting in damp places, and spacious

scissors

rod fastens to waistcoat to leave hands free

landing net

Fishing waistcoat

enough to be worn with a fishing waistcoat underneath.

The fishing waistcoat (Americans call it a vest) is a zip-fronted garment with lots of little pockets down the front. In warm weather it is worn as the main cover, with perhaps the addition of a lightweight nylon jacket when the temperature cools towards the end of the day.

Some waistcoats (also jackets) are fitted with a metal ring or clip to carry a collapsible landing-net on the hip, and also an arrangement for holding the rod fixed to the side of the chest when it is not in use.

Waterproof overtrousers are a *must* in the tackle bag for rainy days.

Thigh waders are required so often when fishing that the keen angler would find it difficult to manage without a pair. Studded soles are safer than rubber cleated soles for climbing over wet stones and down grassy slopes.

To maintain waders in good condition, it is advisable to hang them upside down from special clasps, in a cool corner well away from direct light. Rubber waders stowed in a hot room or regularly folded over will soon deteriorate, especially along the lines of the folds. Waders should be bought a size larger than shoe size to take a thick pair of socks or warm bootliners.

Although reservoir anglers frequently stand in the water to cast, it is worth bearing in mind that trout move close to shore during the night, and that investigating undisturbed water from dry land before wading out in the morning offers the chance to catch fish which otherwise would be scared off before the first cast is made.

Sombre clothing and careful use of bankside growth enables the angler to remain undetected. Heavy-footed movements and shadows across the water should be avoided (*Peter Wheat*)

Safety precaution: It is not advisable to wear waders when boat fishing. They become a serious hazard to life if the boat sinks or if one falls over the side.

Two hats are best. A warm, waterproof one for inclement weather, and a lightweight one with a large peak for hot days.

Dark clothes (browns and greens) blend well with the natural colours of the countryside, and assist the angler considerably in remaining out of sight from fish. It is not, of course, always vital to be soberly dressed to catch fish, but it is certainly commonsense to dress for the occasions when it *may* make a difference between success and failure.

Buying tackle and clothing

Ideally, fly-fishing kit should be purchased from shops which *specialize* in this branch of the sport—

establishments where sound advice is always readily available.

Usually, an individual's choice of tackle is influenced by the type of fly fishing which is available locally, and therefore the local tackle dealer, providing he is himself an experienced fly angler, is the man most qualified to assist in selecting a balanced outfit to suit the individual, the price he can afford, and the waters he will be fishing most often.

Mail-order buying, generally speaking, is not a satisfactory alternative to the tackle shop, but one postal firm I can recommend from personal experience is Nether Wallop Mill, Stockbridge, Hampshire. Headed by Dermot Wilson, expert game angler and author of *Fishing the Dry Fly*, the Mill provides a mail-order fly-fishing service which is second to none—backed by an efficient advisory panel to whom customers can write for in-depth answers to their tackle queries.

7: CASTING THE FLY

Fly casting is not something which can be learned from just the written word alone. It takes practice, more practice, and yet more practice to perfect— preferably under the eye of an experienced caster who is able to isolate faults and correct them before they become habits that are difficult to eradicate later on.

Casting schools are operated from time to time by tackle firms, fishery managements, and local clubs and councils, and these are usually well worth the enrolment fee. Tutors are chosen not only because they are acknowledged experts, but also because they have an all-important flair for passing on their knowledge to others in a manner which is easily understood.

My firm belief is that a few hours of in-depth practical instruction are worth months of reading, and therefore, the following notes are intended only to be the briefest introduction to casting techniques.

I suggest that the complete novice uses a lawn or a close-cropped field as a casting area to begin with, and then graduates to a pond or lake. Markers, placed on the ground or in the water, are used to judge distance and accuracy. Rubber rings are ideal for this purpose. When practising, the line is fitted with a length of level monofilament as a leader (to prevent the tip fraying) and an old fly with the point and barb snipped off.

Never practise casting on abrasive surfaces (concrete, gravel, etc.) as this will quickly damage the skin of the fly line.

The overhead cast

The rod is held in the hand which the individual feels is most natural to cast with. I will assume this

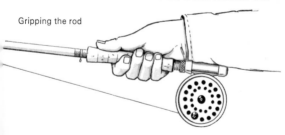

Gripping the rod

to be the right hand. The grip is firm but not over-tight, and the thumb rests on the cork pointing up the length of the rod. The other hand, the left hand in this case, fingers the line just above the reel.

Check at this stage that the reel is fixed on the rod with the handle pointing across the body (to be turned with the free hand when playing a fish), and that line, when pulled off the reel, turns the drum in a clockwise direction.

A position is taken up facing the intended direction of the cast, legs slightly apart and left foot slightly forward. Approximately 6 yd (5·5 m) of line is stripped from the reel and flicked out through the rings to lie in a straight line away from the casting position.

Now the first stage of the back cast is attempted by lifting the rod smartly towards the shoulder to bring the line from front to rear. This action is carried with forearm movement only. The upper arm is held close to the body throughout.

After this simple drill has been repeated a few times, it is improved by concentrating on lifting the rod smoothly to 11 o'clock, quickening the lift between 11 o'clock and 12 o'clock, and, as the 12 o'clock position is reached, bringing the rod a little past this angle with an abrupt back-flick of the wrist. This routine should then be further practised with more line out beyond the rod tip.

It is important that forearm, wrist and rod operate as one firm length until the back-flick is executed—at which point the wrist will be arched downwards. The flick, a crisp snap, removes this arch, but it must not be allowed to bend the wrist further the opposite way than the line of the forearm. Wrist and forearm keep a straight line up the back of the arm, up the thumb and up the rod, and this line should never pass further back than slightly past 12 o'clock.

If it does, the fishing line is liable to drop low behind and catch foliage or hit against the back as it is brought forward again. A painful hook in the ear can result from a dropped back cast, so be warned!

Note, that as the rod is lifted into the back cast, its upper section bends downwards to the weight of the line coming on. This bend increases as the rod moves through the casting arch, building up the springy desire of the rod to force back to the straight. As movement of the rod quickens from 11 o'clock onwards, this power overcomes the weight of the line until, finally, as the back-flick is made, it is boosted enough to accelerate the line backwards—looping out above the tip as the rod also begins to bend backwards.

As the belly of the narrow loop deepens and takes in more and more line, so its weight and speed increases—culminating in cast and fly turning over and becoming fully extended straight behind. When the full force of this straightening out comes on, the line will be felt tugging at the rod top. It can be observed to do so by turning the head over the right shoulder. This tug signifies completion of the back cast.

It is helpful to imagine during the progress of the back cast how the loop is deepening behind, then hooking, and finally turning the cast and fly over. The longer the length of line aerialized, the greater must be the pause between the back cast and the forward cast to allow for looping, turn over and straightening.

This pause must be gauged accurately. If it is delayed too long, momentum will be lost and the line will fall behind. If it is judged too short, the fly will be rushed over so fast [the tip of a fly line travels at over 100 miles (160 km) an hour on back and forward casts] that it will snap off with a crack

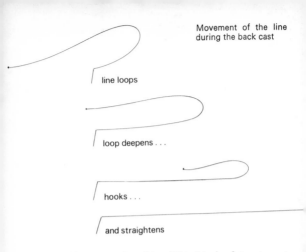

Movement of the line during the back cast

line loops

loop deepens . . .

hooks . . .

and straightens

like a lion tamer's whip. This kind of treatment should be avoided at all cost, as it quickly damages the skin of the line around the tip section.

So then, as the tug of straightened line is felt, the forearm urges the rod forward with increasing acceleration, increasing its tension and that of the line. Between 12 o'clock and 11 o'clock the wrist is brought forward fast into a downward arch, and again a narrow loop, this time moving forward, forms in the line above the rod, deepens, hooks, and turns the fly—completing the forward cast.

Without allowing the fly to alight on the ground or water, the forward cast can be continued into a second back cast, then into a second forward cast, and so on, *ad infinitum*. This action, known as 'false casting', is an excellent means of improving casting style. It should be practised regularly.

In doing so, an attempt should be made to give

PLATE 1

A beautifully marked 4½ lb (2 kg) brown trout from Lough Mask, Ireland (*Bill Howes*)

(*above*) Superbly conditioned rainbow trout weighing 6 lb (2·7 kg) (*Bill Howes*)

Outstanding 11 lb 5½ oz (5·1 kg) brown trout taken by Brian Bates from Grafham Water, Cambridgeshire (*Brian Bates*)

PLATE 2

Stew-grown trout
are stocked in
many waters as
sport for anglers
(*Bill Howes*)

Frequent practice,
the only way to
master casting skills
(*Bill Howes*)

The author displays
a 4¼ lb (1·9 kg)
rainbow caught from
a Test sidestream
(*Peter Wheat*)

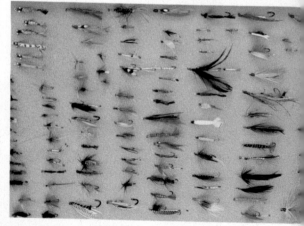

PLATE 3

(*top*) Equipment and colourful materials of the fly tyer
(*Bill Howes*)
(*above*) Random selection of the countless artificial flies
used to catch game and coarse fish (*Bill Howes*)

PLATE 4

Dace, lively little
shoal fish suitable
as quarry for
fly fishing
(*Bill Howes*)

Reed-loving
rudd, when
grown big, are
a first-class
target for fly
methods
(*Bill Howes*)

Chub, like
this specimen
from the
Thames, res-
pond well to
artificial flies
(*Bill Howes*)

PLATE 5

Geoffrey Bucknall holds a big roach which fell for a March Brown (*Bill Howes*)

Mick Nicholls with a 2¼ lb (1 kg) reservoir perch taken on a Missionary lure worked deep (*Bob Church*)

PLATE 6

Hunting lake
trout from
bank and
boat in
calm-water
conditions
(*Bill Howes*)

Fishermen
line the bank
of a popular
fly-only trout
fishery
(*Bill Howes*)

PLATE 7

Moment of truth: a fighting trout safe in the net (*Bill Howes*)

Hazard: a wire fence becomes a problem as a sea trout powers downstream on the Dorset Stour (*Bill Howes*)

Excitement: Fred J. Taylor strives to control a big rainbow hooked in a small carrier stream (*Al Pond*)

PLATE 8

Typical stony stream where trout inhabit the pockets of water between the rocks (*Bill Howes*)

Evening on a Scottish stream – casting wet fly down and across for trout and grayling (*Ray Forsberg*)

Success: Bob Church with a brace of Grafham rainbows topping 4 lb (1·8 kg) each (*Bob Church*)

the back cast a slightly convex curve out to the side, and at the same time to keep the forward cast absolutely straight. Routing the line on separate back and forward paths avoids the possibility of the line hitting against the rod as it is trajected forwards.

To increase line for a longer cast, line is pulled from the reel with the left hand during the back cast, held until the forward cast is nearing completion, and is then released to be drawn through the rings by the weight of line already aerialized. This is known as 'shooting line', and to increase distance still further (eventually, if more line is aerialized than can be handled, it will fall to the ground or land in a heap around the caster's head) false casting is kept up, and more and more line let out with each circuit of the rod through the air.

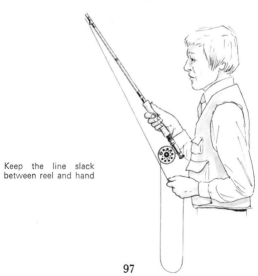

Keep the line slack
between reel and hand

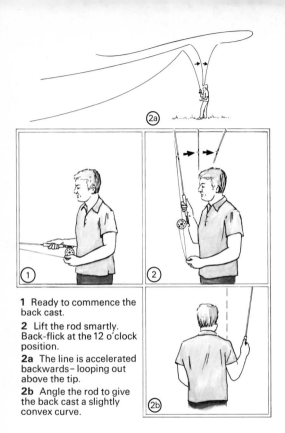

1 Ready to commence the back cast.

2 Lift the rod smartly. Back-flick at the 12 o'clock position.

2a The line is accelerated backwards – looping out above the tip.

2b Angle the rod to give the back cast a slightly convex curve.

Basic overhead casting

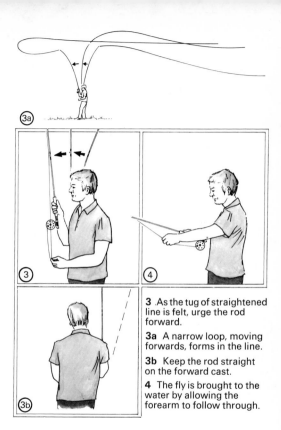

3 As the tug of straightened line is felt, urge the rod forward.

3a A narrow loop, moving forwards, forms in the line.

3b Keep the rod straight on the forward cast.

4 The fly is brought to the water by allowing the forearm to follow through.

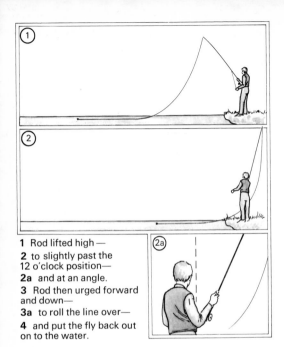

1 Rod lifted high —
2 to slightly past the 12 o'clock position —
2a and at an angle.
3 Rod then urged forward and down —
3a to roll the line over —
4 and put the fly back out on to the water.

Simple roll casting

As soon as the length of line aerialized is considered right for distance, the fly is brought to the water by allowing the forearm to follow through, lowering the rod tip as the line extends forward. When casting for accuracy, such as to a rising fish, the fly is aimed at a spot in the air about 12 in (30 cm) directly above where it will meet the surface, so that it falls lightly on target.

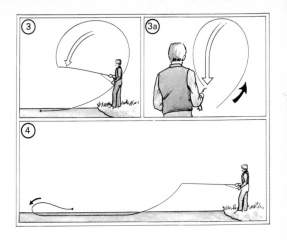

I have suggested that the upper arm be retained close to the body for the overhead cast, but this is a detail which becomes of less importance once the various movements are understood and co-ordinated. Every caster eventually develops an individual style using the forearm or the whole arm as found most comfortable and efficient. It is important that the line between reel and left hand is slack enough to allow the rod to be worked smoothly.

Once one has become reasonably competent at overhead casting, it is then a relatively simple matter to employ the same set of movements to cast with the rod held at different angles in places where a straightforward cast is impossible or difficult: from beneath overhanging boughs, to a fish resting under low foliage, up a heavily bushed channel, and so on. Correct timing, in all circumstances, is achieved by letting the rod do most of the work.

Roll casting, at its simplest, is a short-distance technique used to put a fly back out quickly when it has been part-retrieved and a fish surfaces in a different area of the water. It is also used where bushes or trees are so close behind that they would catch an orthodox back cast.

The rod is lifted high and slightly past the 12 o'clock position to 'sag' the line. Then it is urged forward and down—finishing the motion with a sharp flick of the wrist, to travel the fly in a circular movement back out over the water.

Casting with forward-taper and shooting-head lines

These lines are mainly used across large lakes and reservoirs—waters where long-distance casting is often a priority consideration.

A forward-taper line consists of a heavy 30 ft (9 m) head section spliced into thin shooting line. Distance is gained by false casting the head out to just beyond the rod tip and then shooting the backing line. A few top-rank casters can, under favourable circumstances, cast a full forward-taper line completely off the reel, but such ability is quite exceptional to say the least.

Average casters find a shooting-head backed by flat monofilament a much easier outfit for long casting. The special casting style is carried out as follows:

Assuming that the rod is held in the right hand, the stance is legs slightly apart, feet angled somewhat to the right of the casting direction, and left foot forward.

False casts put rather more than half the shooting-head through the rings, and then the remainder of the shooting-head, plus 30 ft (9 m) of backing line is stripped from the reel to fall at the feet. Now false casting recommences to work out the whole of the shooting-head through the fingers of the left hand until it is 3 ft (90 cm) beyond the rod tip.

This is an aggressive form of casting, with the whole arm and shoulder being used to develop power. The rod is lifted high, slightly above the head, and brought back fast to the 12 o'clock position beyond the shoulder. It is stopped there by tensing the muscles momentarily, and then it is allowed to drift to the 1 o'clock position—never further back than that.

After the usual pause to allow the line to straighten (easily judged because the length of aerialized line is always the same when casting with a shooting head outfit) the rod is punched forward, first with the shoulder, then with the shoulder and arm combined, until the arm is fully extended at shoulder level. As this position is reached, the rod is tipped ahead at speed by pushing the thumb against the handle and turning the wrist downwards. The movement is stopped dead at the 10 o'clock position, and the backing line let go from the free hand.

If the sequence is timed correctly, the shooting-head will fly out fast and straight until all the stripped backing line has been taken up—a distance of nearly 20 yd (18 m) in this example.

Longer casts are achieved by stripping off more backing line, and by double-hauling—pulling the line hard with the left hand on the back and forward casts to increase its velocity.

The first haul is carried out during the back cast, just prior to the rod being stopped in the 12 o'clock position. The left hand drags the line down

1 The first haul is made just prior to the 12 o'clock position.

2 As the line straightens behind, the left hand (holding the line) is moved towards the right shoulder.

Double-hauling

viciously to send it singing out behind. As this is happening, so the left (still clutching the line) is gradually raised to a position near the right shoulder. The second down-haul takes place towards the conclusion of the forward cast, as the rod is being tipped ahead.

Double-hauling speeds-up the whole casting sequence. It takes concentration, quick reflexes, and lots of practice to perform it perfectly, but it is worth mastering as it produces casts of 30–35 yd (27–32 m) consistently.

Shooting-head casting requires a certain amount of strength in wrist, arm and shoulder, combined with a neat style and split-second timing. Brute force alone is not enough.

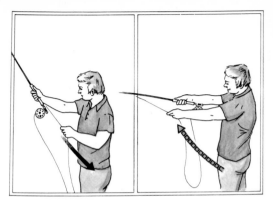

3 The second haul is made as the rod is being tipped ahead.

4 Loose line runs out through the fingers.

Don't put the shooting-head further than 3 ft (90 cm) beyond the rod tip. Don't false cast more than is absolutely necessary. Don't bring the rod back beyond the 1 o'clock position on the back cast. Don't tip the rod over on the forward cast before it has been pushed ahead to the full extent of the arm. Don't commence the forward cast before the line is felt pulling tight on the back cast. Don't let the rod hand drop lower than shoulder height on the forward cast before the fly and line have reached water.

Do let the line go out on the first forward movement after a good back cast. Get the back cast right and the rest will follow naturally. Above all, practise often.

Long-casting is tiring activity, and over a period of several hours it can sap the energy and reduce casting distance considerably, owing to a tendency when tired to rely more on force and less on style. The answer when this is happening, as happen it will, is to cease casting completely for a short while.

Wind Knots

These little gremlins, which form mysteriously in the leader during casting, are certain tackle-weakeners. They tend to occur less frequently as casting ability improves, but they can never be eliminated completely. *Check for them at regular intervals and carefully remove any found with a needle.*

Remove wind knots

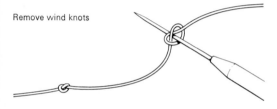

Retrieving

To pick a dry fly off the water, it must first be brought back near enough to the angler to be lifted smoothly into a back cast without putting the rod under excessive strain. This is carried out by retrieving line with the forefinger and thumb of the free hand through a gap formed by pressing the forefinger of the rod hand against the cork. Or, alternatively, gathering it figure-of-eight style into the palm of the free hand.

Sub-surface flies are retrieved by either figure-of-eighting the line or pulling the line through the fingers. When doing it the latter way, the forefinger of the rod hand should grip the line tightly against

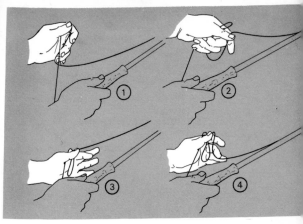

The figure-of-eight retrieve

the cork each time the free hand is brought forward for a new movement, so that should a take occur 'out of the blue', the hook will still find enough resistance to penetrate deeply.

Nymphs and pupae are either twitched ultra-slowly or animated by fast or slow pulls with pauses between each movement. Traditional wet flies and lures are retrieved at fast, medium or slow speeds, according to individual pattern and the feeding mood of the fish.

Line Trays and Pouches

An enormous amount of backing line has to be retrieved when long-distance casting with shooting-head tackle. Dropped on the bank it tangles with herbage, and dropped in the water it snags or drifts away—or worse still drifts away and then snags.

Pouch retainer

Line retainers answer this problem. Some are rafts designed to be attached to the angler; others are pouches worn in front or to the side, at waist level. Pouch retainers are the more versatile of the two types. They can be used when standing on dry land as well as when wading.

Before retrieving *into* a retainer, the first half a dozen feet (1·8 m) of line should be dropped *outside* to provide enough slack to lift the rod high for the next cast without upsetting the coils.

Upstream dry-fly fishing. The angler has crawled into position and is seated to prevent a silhouette against the sky (*Peter Wheat*)

8: PRESENTING THE FLY: RIVERS

Dry-fly fishing

For trout rising to a hatch of fly, the most obvious imitation is a dry floater of a pattern resembling the natural insect.

The orthodox approach to a rising fish is from a downstream position, with the cast made upstream to a spot in the water slightly above the quarry. The fish will be lying in the stream facing the current, watching the surface for insects drifting downstream, and by moving slowly and quietly, keeping low on the bank, using background growth to prevent a silhouette against the light of the sky, and (taking into consideration that a long cast should never be attempted where a short one will do) by not coming too close to the fish, the downstream position will be found to offer the best chance of remaining unobserved.

The tackle required is a full floating line, a floating or quick-sink leader, and a dry fly treated with floatant. Incidentally, some floating lines are purposely designed with extra-fine tips to *break through* the surface and project only a minimum of shadow 'thickness' across the bottom of the stream. On no account should a line of this type be greased to 'improve' its tip-buoyancy.

Although the intention is to drop the fly on the water only about 2 ft (60 cm) above the fish, line is aerialized to reach the fly about 6 ft (1·8 m) above the fish in a *straight line*. This difference in length is required to overcome drag.

Drag, as quickly will be discovered, is the number one curse of the river fisherman. It results from the vagaries of the current bending the line this way and that, making it move here quickly and there slowly, so that the fly behaves unnaturally. It skates the surface, skittering along more quickly than the speed of the water beneath it, and acts altogether quite differently from the unencumbered natural insect.

This, then, is drag, and it is overcome by dropping the line and cast snakily, with the fly settled some

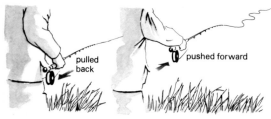

Method of snaking line on a short cast. (On a long cast the rod is angled high and line snaked by pulling and pushing the top)

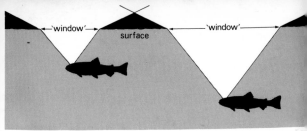

Cone of vision

2 ft (60 cm) above the fish and a trifle towards the angler's bank.

To make a snake cast, line is first worked out in the normal way, and then, on delivery of the forward cast as the line begins to drop, the rod is pulled back and pushed forward with just enough movement to shorten the casting length by zigzagging the end of the line and the leader. These curves 'cushion' slight changes in the speed and direction of the current, and allow the fly a completely unhindered passage over the fish.

Accurate snake casting is never a simple, straightforward procedure. There are differences in distance between the angler and the fish, the position of the fish in relation to the bank, the location of weedbeds and snags, and the direction and strength of any wind which might be blowing, to contend with—all of them factors which can make it harder or easier to present a fly accurately enough to deceive the quarry.

A fish, looking upwards, sights through a 'cone of vision' which, because water refracts the rays of light, greatly increases in area above the surface. The deeper in the water its position, the larger will be the roundel of the surface—the window—through which it sees into the terrestrial world above. How-

Presenting the fly. Left: to a fish lying shallow. Right: to a fish lying deep

ever, this does not mean that a fish lying near the bottom in deep water is easier to catch on a floating fly because it can see more and there is less need to present the fly accurately. On the contrary, there is *always* need for an accurate presentation, no matter at what level a 'marked down' fish is lying.

A cast to a fish which is lying near the surface or in very shallow water should be angled to bring the fly downstream over its head and *directly across* its small window. Whereas, a cast to a fish resident in deep water hugging close to the bottom, should travel the fly down on its *near side*, so that only the fly and a very small amount of the leader appears in its much larger window.

Direct contact with a fly coming downstream towards the angler is maintained by gathering the line with the free hand as it falls slack on the surface —but at the same time taking care not to do this so fast that it interferes with the action of the fly.

After the fly has floated past the fish, it should be allowed to travel well downstream before it is retrieved by figure-of-eighting part of the line and lifting the remainder from the water into a back cast. Apart from there being less chance of scaring the fish if the fly is allowed to drift far below its position, this ploy allows the fish time to drop back on its tail or turn downstream to intercept the fly.

Once the fly is out of the water, false casting across the water *below* the fish is carried out to remove droplets of water clogging the fly, and then it is presented once more by shooting out the line held in the hand.

When a take occurs, the fly may be seized violently or sipped gently, or there may be no more indication than a lift of the surface beneath the fly and its 'quick-as-a-flash' disappearance from view.

The automatic reaction to swing the rod over the shoulder the moment the fly is taken must be resisted at all cost. It too often can result in a fish being pricked but not hooked firmly enough to hold. And the chances are that a pricked fish will

A trout takes a dry fly. It is vital to time the strike correctly to set the hook securely (*George Armit*)

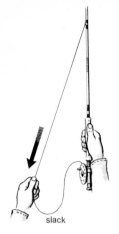

Slack prevents reel-drag when moving the hook on the strike

slack

cease rising for several hours or more. Indeed, a big old fish may not rise again for several days with enough confidence to be deceived by an artificial fly, which at best is a poor substitute for the living insect it is intended to resemble.

To make a strike, pause briefly to give the fish time to turn down with the fly, and then set the hook by tightening the line with a firm lift of the rod and, at the same time, pulling the line sideways and slightly backwards with the free hand to move the hook more quickly. Slack line between the reel and that hand is essential to prevent drag on the reel during this movement.

An alternative approach, when a fish lying close to the near bank proves awkward to reach with an upstream cast, is known as cross-country casting. This is carried out by moving inland to a position directly opposite where the fish is seen rising, and

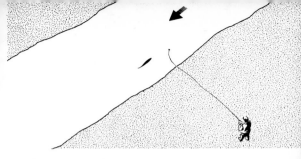
Cross-country casting

from there casting across the bank to drop the fly just upstream of the fish. A certain amount of luck is needed for the fly to be taken before drag sets in and ruins the presentation.

Although upstream casting is the most useful approach, circumstances do occur which are better answered by downstream casting. For example, it is best to a fish which is lying in a spot where upstream casting is exceptionally difficult to perform; or to a fish in clear water on a bright day, which more likely will be deceived by a fly which is cast so that no part of the leader comes near before the fly does so.

To prevent drag when casting downstream, the snake cast is again used—aerializing enough line to reach well below the fish, and then zigzagging it 'on the drop' (as described for upstream casting) to settle the fly on the water directly upstream of the fish.

Bad casting leads to clumsy presentation, and this, more often than not, is the number one reason for a dry fly being refused again and again by feeding fish. A further reason may be that the pattern or size of the fly is at fault. For example, it is perfectly possible for two species of fly to be hatching at the same time, and for the fish to be totally pre-occupied with eating the sparser, less obvious (to the angler) insect, to the neglect of the other insect together with the angler's imitation of it!

If the feed-fly cannot be identified, the only answer is to take pot-luck and experiment with a variety of patterns in different sizes.

Nymph fishing

Nymph fishing is worthwhile when there are no flies hatching, when a hatch is in progress but few fish are seen rising and, obviously, when fish are indicating their interest in nymphs by bulging the surface as they twist and turn to take them.

The line for nymph fishing is a full floater. This is matched with a leader which has been greased to within 2–3 ft (60–90 cm) of the point. Suitable nymphs are generalized patterns, preferably weighted with copper wire to make them sink fast.

After the nymph has been cast so as to enter the water far enough above the fish (or where a fish is judged to be lying) to allow space for it to sink, it is worked down with the current by figure-of-eighting line into the free hand. Throughout the cast, the angler must remain alert for the slightest hint that the nymph has been intercepted—which may be indicated by the floating part of the leader sliding under, by a bulge of the surface above where the nymph is moving, by a flash of the fish's flank, or even by the exciting vision of the whole fish as it rushes, jaws agape, to seize the fly.

The strike should be made firmly and quickly, but not with too much force or the leader may break.

Upstream wet-fly fishing

Wet-fly fishing is typical to rivers of the fast-flowing kind, where the water is an ever-changing mixture of stony stickles, bubbling eddies, swirly corners and swift runs squeezing between boulders and slabs. The line for this fishing is a full floater, and the leader either a sinker or a sink-tip floater. Insect-imitating and fancy traditional wet flies are suitable patterns.

The approach is made by walking or wading in an upstream direction, and casting the fly at short range (perhaps no further than two or three times the length of the rod) to rising fish and into likely fish-holding spots. As the fly travels down the current, contact is maintained by collecting the slacking line and by lifting the rod high enough in the air to move the fly a fraction faster than the speed of the current.

Many fish bite so greedily that they will hook themselves, but any indication of a take—no matter how slight—should be reacted to, as countless tweaks and nibbles will occur on days when fish are rising freely.

Downstream wet-fly fishing

The direction of a strong wind can be enough in-fluence to decide between casting a fly up or down the river, but downstream casting is nearly always the better approach on those cold rainy days when fish are skulking dour and unresponsive along the bottom.

Commencing at the top of the fishery, the water is walked or waded and searched with a wet-tip or sinking line cast longishly down and across to swing the fly round with the current. After the line has straightened out directly below, the fly is left wiggling for a few seconds, and is then retrieved in a series of short jerks far enough upstream to be lifted out into the next back cast without overloading the rod.

Special attention should be given to spots where food comes naturally to the fish. For example, by holding several feet of line in the free hand, it is possible to manoeuvre the fly above a likely holt—say a channel between two rocks—and send it hunting deep into the constriction by letting go the spare line at a controlled rate.

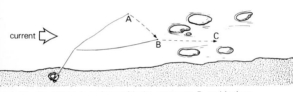

The fly cast to A, swings with the current to B, and is then controlled carefully between the rocks C

A take may come at any stage of the fly's passage: as it swings across, as it trundles through a lie, as it 'hangs' on a straightened line, or as it is being brought upstream.

Downstream wet-fly is standard technique for sea trout. A sea-trout pool which is singled out for night fishing should be trial-tested first during daylight hours, so that its features are thoroughly understood before the time comes to cast into it 'blind'. If a team of flies is to be used, it is worth making up several spare leaders with flies attached to cut down on wasted time when tangles occur—as they often do in the dark.

Fly Teams

I recommend a single-fly presentation for beginners, but with more experience three-fly teams can also be tried when wet-fly fishing, both upstream and downstream. Three different flies are tied on to start with—to be changed later to three flies of whatever pattern is interesting the fish most of all.

Flies for casting downstream have hackles and wings which slope backwards and offer no resistance to the flow, whereas upstream flies, which must be made to work the current, are fashioned with stand-up hackles and wings.

Three-fly team

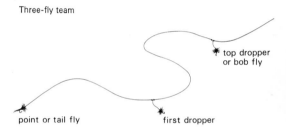

top dropper
or bob fly

point or tail fly

first dropper

The manipulation of a team of flies upstream can be enhanced by tying on a hackled dry pattern as top dropper or bob fly. This fly, as well as attracting fish to itself, rides the roughened current strongly, and by so doing imparts greater movement to the wet flies swirling below.

Sedge fishing

When fish are rising to sedge flies in the evening, there is no better approach to catching them than a floating line outfit armed with a dry or wet imitation. The artificial fly is retrieved by giving the line short pulls to make it scuttle the surface—the typical movement of the natural insect. Takes are usually deliberate and easily connected.

During hatches of mayfly, a sedge pattern sometimes proves more killing than an imitation of the mayfly, and particularly after mayflies have been abundant on the water for many days.

9: PRESENTING THE FLY— STILL-WATERS

The locomotion of aquatic insects through the water varies from one group of insects to the next, and the quickest way of learning how to activate their imitations is to observe their different movements carefully.

For example, the maturing nymphs of upwinged lake flies progress in short darting motions along the bottom and through the weeds, and then swim steadily up to the surface when the time arrives for them to hatch.

The artificial is worked with short jerks along the bottom when there is no hatch in progress, and is sunk deep to be drawn up slowly when flies are hatching and fish are taking nymphs as they approach the surface.

Chironomid pupae travel more slowly up from the bottom, and then 'hang' just beneath the surface prior to their emergence—where they are easy prey for the trout which have followed them up.

Single-fly and three-fly pupae teams are presented on a floating line and a leader greased to within an inch (2·5 cm) of the point fly. The retrieve is carried out with

Chironomid pupae at the surface

*absolute slowness in a series of tiny jerks with long pauses
between each movement.*

Corixae (lesser water boatmen) swim strongly to
the surface.

*The imitation corixa is allowed to sink near to the
bottom, and is then brought back up with a long steady pull.
When it nears the surface it is allowed to fall again to near
the bottom.*

It is advisable to keep on the move when there are
no takes and no fish are seen rising. A useful rig for
'fishing the water' is a floating forward-taper line
matched with a three-fly team on a sinking cast—
pupae on the top and first dropper and a large
nymph on the point. Surface drift assists in moving
the flies, and the angler walks along the bank, in the
same direction as the drift, to keep in touch with the
flies. The strike is made *immediately* a take is felt or
seen.

Should surface drift be travelling directly away
from the bank, across the water, the same three-fly
team can be cast with the wind and then drifted
further out by giving line. Distances of 40 yd (36 m)
or more are possible using this technique.

It is often suggested by writers that trout feeding
on pupae are too preoccupied with these insects to
respond to artificials of larger size. This, however, is

not true of reservoir trout, which will often take a black lure fished deep during a chironomid feast. The stomachs of some of these lure-caught chironomid-eaters have been found to contain both pupae and small fish—indicating their lack of complete preoccupation with either item at the time of capture.

When nymph fishing, a slow-sink or wet-tip line is ideal for searching depths greater than 15 ft (4·5 m), and a floating line for lesser levels.

Lure and Wet-Fly Fishing

Lures and wet flies are fished at every depth, speed and variation of retrieve. The Worm Fly and the Black and Peacock Spider are typical slow flies, while attractors such as Dunkeld, Peter Ross and Butcher, are examples of fast flies. However, there are no hard and fast rules about how particular patterns of fly should be fished. Fast flies regularly catch fish when retrieved slowly, and vice versa.

Lures are perhaps at their deadliest when fish are engaged in eating fry. Fry-feeders should be looked for in the vicinity of tributary stream inlets, boat jetties, dam walls, valve towers, weedy areas and submerged hedges and ditches. Swirls and scattering fry indicate where and when this type of feeding is taking place.

Sedge Fishing

Still-water trout frequently gorge themselves on adult sedge flies during the last hour or two before full darkness. A single-fly presentation avoids the tangles which can so easily occur when fishing a team of flies in poor light, but if more than one fly is used—for example, a dry sedge on the top dropper and wet sedges on the first dropper and point—it is advisable to have a second team of flies rigged and ready to change over to if the first set fouls up. This is far more efficient than attempting to sort out a spoilt leader at a time when fish are feeding ravenously and there is little time remaining in which to catch them.

Sedge larvae imitations, fished deep and slow, can be tried during the day. The Stick Fly is one of the more notable patterns.

Stick Fly

Dry-Fly Fishing
Aquatic flies which are hatching or egg-laying, and terrestrial flies which have been blown on to the water in quantity, entice fish to feed at the surface. An imitative pattern of the predominant insect should be cast to float where the activity of the fish is greatest, and twitched occasionally as additional attraction.

Hot-Spots
Hot-spots are areas where fish gather to feed. The windward side of a reservoir, for example, is always likely to contain shoals attracted by the build-up of natural food in this area. Close attention should be given to bays and corners—and any promontory where a wind lane has formed. Fish moving along wind lanes are often responsive to artificial flies.

Netting a good Lough Mask (Co. Mayo) brown trout.
Hooked during a traditional-style drift, it took the point fly
of a three-fly team (*Irish Tourist Board*)

Boat fishing

Drifting

The traditional loch-style drift is carried out by
taking the boat upwind, positioning it beam-on to
the wind, and letting it drift back downwind. In a
breeze or moderate wind there is need only for an
occasional pull on the oars to redirect the course of
the drift, but in a stiff wind it may be necessary also
to put out a well-designed drogue from a midships
position to reduce the speed of the boat's passage to
a fishable rate.

Two anglers, seated one at each end of the craft,
can fish together quite comfortably on a broadside
drift—both anglers casting downwind ahead of the
course for short distances with teams of three small
wet flies, top droppers dibbling the surface. The

success of this technique stems from the boat's drift continually alighting the flies in fresh areas of water to entice pockets of fish feeding near the surface.

In recent years, an entirely modern style of drift has been developed which has made it possible to fish all levels and along the bottom 'on the move'. This extremely versatile approach is particularly suitable on big reservoirs.

The boat is set to drift bows first by hanging a drogue from the centre of the stern. Two anglers can then cast out over opposite sides and investigate different depths with different techniques. When one angler contacts fish, the other angler straightway changes over to the successful tactics to claim his share of the sport.

At Anchor
Hot-spots far out from the bank (submerged ditches, streams, hedgerows, buildings, etc.) are ideally searched from a boat at anchor.

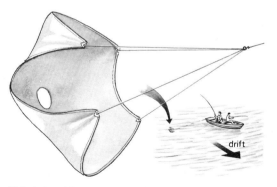

drift

Well-designed drogue and method of use

A bow anchor holds the boat steadily enough to present lures and wet flies, but for nymphs—which must be fished slowly and carefully, with direct contact the whole time—it is desirable to turn the boat into a solid platform by dropping two anchors, one from the bow and the other from the stern.

Never, no matter which fishing method is employed, should the boat be held tight fore and aft in rough weather. The boat will 'lean' and ship water; it may turn turtle. For the same reason, the securing rope should always be attached to the bow when single-hook anchoring, and never from the centre of the gunwale.

Without a doubt, the reservoir angler afloat has considerable advantage over the man on the bank, but it must be borne firmly in mind that it is foolish to tempt fate by leaving the shore without first taking proper safety precautions.

A big reservoir being beaten up by powerful winds is definitely no place for an inexperienced boat-handler out on his own. Such conditions are as dangerous as the open sea.

Check the boat for defects. Ensure that oars, anchors and balers are aboard. Wear a life-jacket. Tell somebody ashore that you are going out, and the approximate time of your return. Don't wear waders. And don't stand up to cast unless the boat is wide-beamed and extremely stable.

Over-cautious? Not at all—not where human life is concerned.

Playing fish

Directly after a fish has been hooked there will be a certain amount of retrieved line to deal with. This loose line is no problem if the fish is a small one [less than $1\frac{1}{2}$ lb (0·6 kg)] because a fish of this class can be played out by simply giving and taking the line with the free hand, and stripping it in for netting without making any use of the reel.

A larger fish, however, is not so easily beaten. It must be played 'off the reel', and to this end it is vital to get all the retrieved line back on the drum without delay.

The fish is first controlled by clutching the line with the fingers of the free hand. But just as soon as possible, this grip is transferred to between thumb and forefinger of the rod hand, so that the free hand is then spare to wind up the retrieved line. In order to provide enough tension to lay the turns firmly on

Winding up retrieved line

apply constant pressure   use sidestrain

Playing action

the drum, I have made a habit of hooking the little finger of the rod hand round the line at the point where it enters the reel.

Should the fish run powerfully off while the retrieved line is being gathered, line is yielded under pressure of the thumb and forefinger of the rod hand. If, however, the fish moves away at an angle which puts a slack bight in the line beyond the rod tip—

If a jumping trout is held too hard it may part the leader as it falls back to the water (*Peter Wheat*)

for example, towards the bank—backward steps should be taken to make the line tight again.

Once the reel is in action, it is then a matter of patiently easing and gaining line until the fish tires and ceases to resist. The line must be kept tight the whole time, with the rod held at an angle of about 45 degrees acting as a cushioning spring and keeping the fish under constant pressure. Any move of the fish towards dangerous snags is countered by swinging the rod over and applying sidestrain to pull it off balance. If the fish jumps, lower the rod top to lessen tension of the line and by so doing counter any 'snatch' which may occur.

Above all, when playing a big fish, stay calm. Attempting to drag it to the net is very unlikely to work. The fish will simply struggle all the harder for freedom, and perhaps snap the leader or straighten the hook. Big fish are invariably stubborn creatures. They must be worn down little by little, not bullied about in an attempt at an early submission.

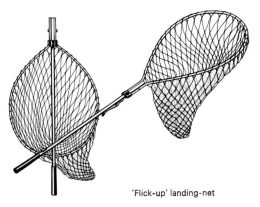

'Flick-up' landing-net

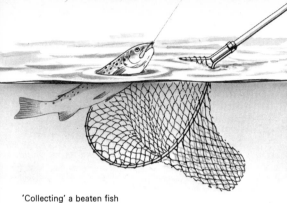

'Collecting' a beaten fish

Landing fish

A strong, reliable landing-net is an essential item of tackle. By far the best type for fly fishing is a collapsible 'flick-up' designed to be carried at the waist, clipped on a belt or jacket ring.

Although a 'flick-up' net is perfectly functional for boat fishing, it is easier to net a fish from a seated position with a rigid landing-net fitted with an angled head-frame. This is the design which regular boat anglers tend to prefer.

The net frame (round and triangular shapes are equally as suitable) should be large enough to cope with big fish, and the handle should be telescopic to provide a range of lengths for different circumstances.

To 'collect' a beaten fish, the landing-net is extended far enough out to submerge the frame completely. It is then held inert while the fish is drawn

Trout expert
Dick Shrive
'collects' a
beaten fish in a
boat-net fitted
with an angled
head-frame
(*Peter Wheat*)

Netting a
beaten fish. The
landing-net is
held still, while
rod pressure
eases the fish
over the rim
(*Peter Rayment*)

over the rim with rod pressure. A smooth lift to engulf the fish in the mesh completes the procedure.

If you ask a fellow angler to net a fish for you, do make sure first that he understands the drill and will carry it out as asked. To avoid any possibility of confusion, leading perhaps to the loss of the fish, the criterion is that the man with the rod controls the man with the net.

The rules of some fisheries state that trout measuring less than a certain length must be returned to the water. To avoid damaging these fish they should, as often as is possible, be unhooked without being removed from the water. This is done by working the fingers of the free hand down the leader, gripping the hook firmly, and twisting it free without actually touching the captive.

Tiddler trout which are hooked so deeply that they have to be netted out should always be handled with wet hands, and placed back in the water rather than thrown in.

Keeping Trout Fresh

Killed trout must be cared for if they are to keep their 'fresh-from-the-water' flavour. It is no good tipping them into a plastic bag and just hoping they will stay sweet, because it is more than likely that they will rapidly deteriorate—particularly in hot weather, or when caught in the morning and not removed until late at night.

Personally, I can recommend an American-style stringer for keeping trout fresh. Stringers are gadgets to which trout are either clipped or threaded and submerged in water. It is the work of half an hour to make a DIY version.

A simple design consists of a 6 in (15 cm) length of thick dowel as a carrying handle, fitted with a screw-eye at each end and a small loop of plastic-

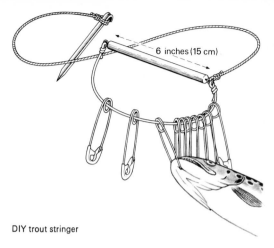

6 inches (15 cm)

DIY trout stringer

coated curtain rail holding a dozen jumbo-size safety-pins. A length of nylon cord, knotted to a metal tent peg, is attached to one of the screw-eyes.

Captured trout are killed, hung on individual pins passed through their lower jaws and secured by the cord in the shallows, or over the side of the boat to keep them cool.

An alternative to a stringer is a reed bag called a bass. The bass is kept well soaked to preserve trout retained within.

For long trips home I normally transfer my catch to a cooler-box containing an ice-pack.

Items for the Tackle Bag

Surgical forceps (now sold in tackle shops) are used to extract the hook when it is located far back in the gullet. When using this instrument, care needs to be

taken, not to damage the delicate organs beneath the gill-covers of fish which are to be returned to the water, and also the dressing of the fly.

A spring-balance is handy for checking the weight of notable-sized trout. Before weighing, kill the fish and then insert the scale-hook through the soft part of its lower jaw.

Trout are at their best for eating when they are cooked at the waterside. A convenient method of doing this is by smoking them. The task takes 20 minutes using a portable smoker which is small enough to fit into the tackle bag, and there is no risk of overcooking.

The Brook's Home Smoker, a suitable unit for anglers who enjoy eating trout straight from the water (*Peter Wheat*)

Identifying Diet

For a great deal of the time trout remain hidden from view deep beneath the surface. It is then necessary to fish for them 'blind' with a favourite pattern worked along the bottom, where most sub-surface feeding takes place.

The aim of this approach is to catch a fish as quickly as possible and, from its stomach contents, discover what items the shoal it came from are feeding on. This information is obtained with the help of either a marrow-scoop or an 'Aymidge' pipette.

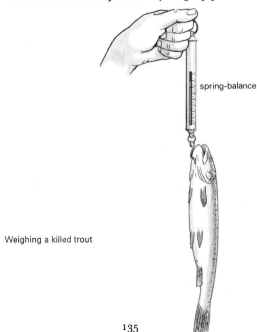

spring-balance

Weighing a killed trout

Marrow-scoop

The marrow-scoop is a special elongated spoon which is inserted down the throat of a fish (after it has been killed, of course) and into its stomach. It is then turned and drawn out with, hopefully, a portion of the stomach contents retained in the scoop.

The more modern pipette, invented by John Aylott, performs the same function, but even more efficiently. Its suction system of operation causes far less damage to fragile insects than does the marrow-scoop.

Stomach contents are placed in a saucer of clean water for identification, and stirred gently to isolate individual creatures.

Whether or not the study is taken further than simplified classifications such as beetle, snail, nymph, sedge larva, etc., depends on the individual. Just a broad ability to 'read' stomach contents can be a tremendous advantage to any angler, but obviously keen students of natural history will wish to take this line of research more seriously by

'Aymidge' pipette

136

consulting specialized reference books.

Another useful aid in diet identification is the nature viewer. This device consists of an observation chamber fitted with a compartment at one end to hold specimens. Looked at through the other end the specimens are seen magnified five times. The nature viewer is a splendid means of identifying live winged insects caught in a collecting net or landing-net.

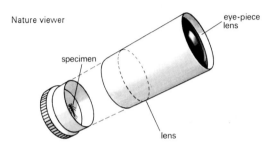

Nature viewer

eye-piece lens

specimen

lens

Trophy Fish

Plaster casts of lunker trout can be made at home by following the instructions given by the late David Carl Forbes in his book *Catch A Big Fish* (Newnes).

If the few materials for the task are stored in advance, it is possible to make a mould of a trout quickly enough on the day of its capture for the carcase to be removed for eating purposes, so preventing the wastage of its valuable flesh.

The difficult part of making a plaster cast is creating a life-like finish. Unless one has a real aptitude for painting fish, the job is best left to a competent artist. A badly painted cast is an eyesore on the wall and anything but a satisfactory reminder of a memorable day's fishing.

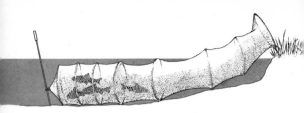

Keepnet

11: COARSE FISH ON FLY

For many years coarse-fish anglers neglected fly fishing in favour of float, leger and spinning methods, but nowadays, as a direct result of the ever-increasing interest in fly fishing for trout, there is a revival in progress of what was once standard practice—the hunting of coarse fish with fly-fishing methods.

Moreover, it has been discovered that as well as acknowledged fly-takers such as bleak, dace, chub, rudd and perch, there are also other coarse species which can be tried with an artificial fly with every chance of success. Already there have been advancements in this area, notably for pike, together with hints of further interesting possibilities still awaiting serious attention.

For example, eels weighing more than 5 lb (2·2 kg) (black lures), bream of double-figure proportions (white lures), and very large carp (nymphs) have been landed in recent seasons by anglers fly fishing for trout. And in fact, so individually big have the coarse species in some trout reservoirs now become, that it can only be a matter of time before at least one or two British coarse-fish records get topped by specimens hooked accidentally (in the mouth) on flies intended for trout. Record-breaking rudd, roach, bream and perch are all possibilities.

The tench is another coarse fish which occasionally crops up in the catch-returns of trout anglers. The superb tench of 5 lb 12 oz (2·6 kg) from the Barcombe Mills stretch of the Sussex Ouse is one such fish. It fell for a Pheasant Tail artificial cast for brown trout, and it took no less than 45 minutes to subdue on a size 14 hook and 3 lb (1·3 kg) leader point. Its captor was Portslade angler Robin West.

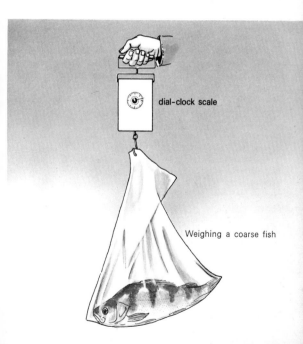

dial-clock scale

Weighing a coarse fish

Coarse fish are not caught to be eaten. The pleasure of catching them comes solely from tempting them to the hook and then playing them to the net. After being weighed, and perhaps photographed too, they are returned to the water to live on and fight again another day.

If coarse fish are to be kept for any length of time they should be retained in a spacious keepnet pegged out along the bottom to allow them plenty of free movement. The only kind of keepnet I would consider for this purpose is one made from knotless material with holes of small diameter. Such a net, unlike the now out-of-date knotted type, does not dislodge protective slime or split fins.

Coarse fish can be weighed individually in a strong plastic bag, and collectively in a keepnet with the bank-stick removed. The weight of the container must obviously be deducted afterwards to arrive at an accurate estimate of the catch-weight. A dial-clock scale is more accurate than a spring-balance, with the added advantage that it can be adjusted to compensate for the weight of the container before the catch is weighed.

Providing the rules allow, waters with high-grown banks—where back casts are forever snagging bushes and trees—are ideally fished from a boat. Early morning and late evening are times to visit overcrowded fisheries, when the presence of other anglers is minimal.

In fly fishing for coarse fish, size of the artificial and careful presentation are infinitely more important factors than exact imitation. Patterns with white in their bodies, or white tail-tags, are especially deadly.

Take extra precautions when casting Regular trout anglers are well aware of the danger of passing too closely behind an angler who is casting a fly, but coarse anglers who are not familiar with the method may not realize just how far inland a back cast reaches. *It is essential to remain alert to people passing behind if serious injury is to be avoided.*

The Grayling

Family THYMALLIDAE   *Thymallus thymallus*
Distribution: Well-oxygenated rivers in England, Wales and Scotland. Also stocked to provide additional variety in a few still-waters.
Quality size: 1 lb (0·45 kg)

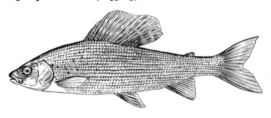

This species is something of a link between game and coarse fish. A member of the salmon family, related to trout, it spawns during the spring at the same time as the coarse species. The arrangement of its fins includes a 'trouty' adipose fin and a long sail-like dorsal fin by which it is immediately identified.

It is the size and shape of the dorsal fin which gives the grayling its unique fighting characteristics on the hook—a stubborn, gyrating resistance, which really makes the angler work hard to beat his fish—whether played in a soft-flowing southern chalk-stream or in a rushing tumbling northern river.

The grayling hugs the bottom and dashes verti-

The large and powerful dorsal fin of the grayling (*Bill Howes*)

cally upwards to take flies and other creatures drifting down through the upper levels and on the surface, and it is probably the speed and the acute angle of the rise which accounts for the fact that the artificial fly is often missed completely. However, this is no problem to the angler, because grayling, when feeding, will come again and again to the fly—providing it is carefully presented with each cast.

Grayling are caught on both dry flies and wet flies of small size. Many patterns have been found suitable, but over the years some of them have proved more successful than others—particularly flies with red, orange, yellow, blue or green in their dressings. Here is a selection of popular patterns: Greenwell's Glory, Snipe and Purple, Black Gnat, Partridge and Orange, Dark Needle Fly, Pheasant Tail, Shrimp, Bradshaw's Fancy, Brunton's Fancy, Sturdy's Fancy, Rolt's Witch, Terry's Terror, Grayling Steel Blue, Orange Otter, Green Insect,

Treacle Parkin, Red Tag, Bumble flies—Orange,
Yellow and Mulberry varieties, etc.

Both upstream and downstream tactics will catch
grayling, and the most important thing to remember is to remain completely alert the whole time,
ready to strike the moment the fly is intercepted and
before the fish has a chance to eject it.

Although unloved and destroyed in 'trout-only'
waters, the grayling is acknowledged to be an outstanding sporting species by discerning anglers. Not
only is it one of the most beautiful of the British fish,
but it is also obliging. It indulges in hectic bouts of
feeding in all kinds of weather, and may even be
found willing to respond to dry fly in the depths of
winter.

The Bleak

Family CYPRINIDAE   *Alburnus alburnus*
Distribution: Rivers in England and eastern Wales.
Also found less commonly in lakes and ponds.
Quality size: A 2 oz (56 g) bleak is a veritable giant
of its kind.

Bleak do not grow large enough to offer sport for
ordinary coarse fishing methods, and are seriously
fished for only by youngsters and matchmen. However, they do offer an interesting subject for fly
fishing on hot summer days when they are shoaled
actively near the surface. A floating line matched
with a finely pointed leader and a tiny dry midge

fly is a suitable outfit for this work.

Greedy and free-rising, bleak must be struck ultra-fast to make contact. Indeed, any angler who can catch bleak consistently need never fear that his reflexes will not be responsive enough to deal with any other species found in British waters.

The Dace

Family CYPRINIDAE *Leuciscus leuciscus*
Distribution: Widespread in rivers of England and eastern Wales. Restricted in Ireland to the Cork Blackwater and its tributaries. Also found occasionally in ponds and lakes.
Quality size: 6–8 oz (170–226 g)

Dace are small-growing, fast-biting shoal fish. They rise eagerly in warm weather, and occasionally also in winter. In my opinion, dry-fly fishing is the most pleasurable method of catching them. Proven patterns include: Gold-Ribbed Hare's Ear, Olive Dun, Red Tag, Coachman, Black Gnat, Alder, Greenwell's Glory and Wickham's Fancy.

Dace are also caught on tiny attractor flies, lures, pupae and nymphs. A team of three flies—dry fly on the top dropper and wet flies or nymphs on the first dropper and the point—is a rig favoured by

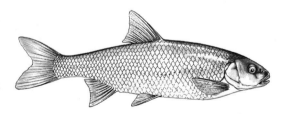

some anglers, but my preference is for a single fly presented on a 2–3 lb (0·9–1·3 kg) leader point.

When takes are being missed continually, probably either the strike is too slow or the fly is too big. Dace are small-mouthed fish, and this often prevents them sucking in a large, stiff-hackled pattern—particularly in fast-water lies. A change to a fly of smaller size with a softer hackle usually improves the hooking rate.

During a heavy hatch of fly, a shoal of dace may feed so selectively that they will steadfastly refuse to take anything but an exact imitation of the natural insect. Fortunately, such occasions are rare events along most rivers.

Among notable dace caught on fly is a leash from the river Cam to the rod of Richard Walker. Three fish weighing between 1 lb 1 oz (0·4 kg) and 1 lb 5 oz (0·5 kg) which fell for a Black Gnat on successive casts.

The Chub

Family CYPRINIDAE *Leuciscus cephalus*
Distribution: Indigenous to rivers in most parts of England and southern Scotland. Also found in a few lakes.
Quality size: 3 lb (1·3 kg)

The chub is the largest coarse fish regularly

caught on fly. Notable specimens include a Thames chub of 7 lb 5 oz (3·3 kg) which fell for a size 6 Coch-y-Bonddu in a backwater at Marlow, and chub of 7 lb 14 oz (3·5 kg) and 7 lb 8 oz (3·4 kg) from the Dorset Stour in 1937 and 1949 respectively. The earlier fish of the two took a Butcher.

Because of the possibility of hooking trophy-size fish when chub hunting, it is not a good idea to use a leader point of less than 4 lb (1·8 kg) test—even as heavy as 6 lb (2·7 kg) in a river known to contain really big chub.

Chub respond to small lures, wet flies, and exotic bug patterns such as the Aquatic Spider—a strange-looking fly which does remarkably well on some days. However, a big bushy dry fly, cast into fast shallows, smooth runs, eddying side-pools, and the quiet glides which pass darkly beneath overhanging foliage, is by far the most productive imitation for these fish.

Alder, Coachman, Coch-y-Bonddu, Red Tag, Palmers—Soldier and Black varieties—and Zulu, tied on size 8 hooks, are recommended patterns.

Casting to individual fish lying in clear water is fraught with problems and disappointment. Often

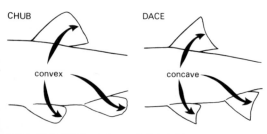

Points of identification between chub and dace

a single cast creates enough disturbance to send the intended victim bolting into the thickest cover it can find, never to be seen again on that day. At the same time though, when everything does work out according to plan, the sight of a brassy old chub rising leisurely to slurp in an artificial is a memory which never dims. Just one such experience is ample compensation for the dozens of bungled attempts which led up to it.

Small chub and big dace can be told apart by the trailing-edge shape of the dorsal, pelvic and anal fins. The edges of these fins are convex in chub and concave in dace.

The Rudd

Family CYPRINIDAE   *Scardinius erythropthalmus*
Distribution: Still-waters, slow rivers and canals in England and Ireland.
Quality size: England 1 lb (0·45 kg), Ireland 1 lb 8 oz (0·68 kg)

Although this species indulges in spells of bottom feeding, its protruding lower lip declares it to be mainly an upper-levels feeder.

Rudd shoals like to have plenty of cover near

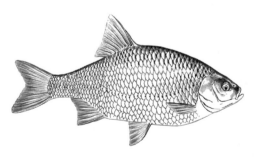

them, and they should therefore be looked for during the summer and autumn months in places where beds of weed, reed, rush and lily grow profusely. To the best of my knowledge, rudd are not worth hunting with fly tackle after dropping water temperatures have sent them deep for the winter period.

Surface-feeding rudd can be tempted with tiny dry and wet flies mounted on a greased leader of 3–4 lb (1·3–1·8 kg) point strength. When rudd are absent from the surface, a white and gold nymph twitched along between 3 and 18 in (7·6–45 cm) sub-surface is a method worth trying. Also worth trying is a flashy wet fly on an ungreased leader brought back in short bursts with long pauses between movements.

Boat fishing enables more of a big water to be searched than would otherwise be possible, and is a means of approaching awkwardly placed shoals from the best angle and distance. Large rudd are shy elusive creatures, less likely to be frightened off when cast to from long range.

In some trout reservoirs there are rudd which average nearly 2 lb (0·9 kg). They make fine alternative sport for anglers who appreciate their quality, but more often than not they get treated as vermin simply because they are rudd and not trout. A very silly attitude, in my opinion.

The roach, *Rutilus rutilus*, a species closely similar to the rudd, is also responsive to fly-fishing methods. A notable capture, for example, was the 2¼ lb (1 kg) roach taken on a lure from Grafham Reservoir, Cambridgeshire, in 1974 by Bob Church. Shustoke Reservoir, West Midlands, is another fly-only trout water which has yielded 2 lb (0·9 kg) class roach to fly-fishing methods [as well as perch over 3 lb (1·3 kg) and bream over 9 lb (4 kg)].

Fred J. Taylor, twitching a nymph along a reedy margin on a hot summer's day . . .

was rewarded with this plump specimen-size rudd (*Fred J. Taylor*)

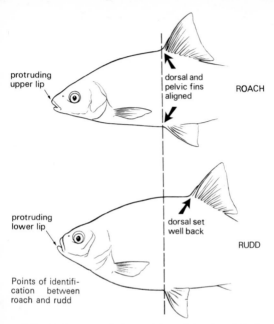

protruding
upper lip

dorsal and
pelvic fins
aligned

ROACH

protruding
lower lip

dorsal set
well back

RUDD

Points of identifi-
cation between
roach and rudd

Mouth shape, and the position of the dorsal fin in
relation to the pelvic fins, tell rudd and roach apart
more certainly than colour. This is particularly true
of immature fish.

The Perch

Family PERCIDAE   *Perca fluviatilis*
Distribution: Common to waters of every type.
England, Ireland, southern Scotland and parts of
Wales.
Quality size: 1 lb (0·45 kg)

Fly fishing for perch is exceptionally productive in still-waters. And indeed, there are times when perch are so numerous in certain trout reservoirs, that it is more difficult *not* to hook them when unwittingly casting into an area they have taken over as a feeding station.

Perch attack lures, wet flies and nymphs, but lures are by far the most productive patterns. Richard Walker, who has numerous 2 lb (0·9 kg) plus perch to his credit, has designed a special tandem lure pattern for this species which he calls the Hanningfield Lure (after Hanningfield Reservoir near Chelmsford). It has proved a highly successful creation for enticing big perch in many of the waters where it has been tried.

The Pike

Family ESOCIDAE   *Esox lucius*
Distribution: Waters of all kinds—most parts of Britain and Ireland.
Quality size: 5 lb (2·2 kg) rivers. 8 lb (3·6 kg) still-waters

During the 1975 trout season, Bob Church accidentally caught a pike while fly fishing from a boat

on Grafham Reservoir. It took a Jack Frost white marabou lure being retrieved close to the bottom in 18 ft (5·4 m) of water, and put up a tremendous fight against ordinary-strength reservoir tackle. At 20 lb 4 oz (9·1 kg) (only 6 years old) it ranks as one of the biggest authenticated pike ever taken on fly from a British water.

Anybody who has ever hooked a biggish pike on a fly rod will be well aware of the fun and thrills which resulted from trying to beat it—even if a trout was the real target of operations at the time! And so it comes as no surprise to me that the serious pursuit of pike with fly rod and lures gains new converts with the passing of each season.

Bob Church poses with the 20 lb 4 oz (9·1 kg) pike he caught from Grafham Reservoir on a Jack Frost lure (*Bob Church*)

It is not a modern method, however, and in fact, as long ago as 1662, Col. Robert Venables recorded in his book, *The Experienced Angler:*

'I know some who do angle for Bream and Pike with artificial flies, but I judge the labour lost and the knowledge a needless curiosity, those fish being taken much easier (especially the pike) by other wayes.'

Despite the good colonel's pessimism, the method has continued to enjoy a fair degree of popularity right down through the centuries to the present day.

In the latter half of the 19th century, for example, catching pike on large feather lures was a favourite sport in Ireland. And in the beginning years of this century, Sir Courtney Boyle, while presiding at one of the annual dinners of the Fly Fishers' Club, was sufficiently familiar with the approach to be able to remark (tongue in cheek I suspect) that: 'A fly is one of the best baits for pike you can possibly have, whether in a river, lake or brook.'

Pike lures (*Peter Wheat*)

Streamer lure

As far as modern times are concerned, pike fishing with fly tackle has been almost totally neglected in Britain. In America and Germany though, it has become firmly established as a major sport-fishing technique.

German pike-expert, Ekkehard Wiederholz, described it as: 'One of the most exciting methods of fishing I know, and well worth the extra effort.'

American writer Tom McNally who, like Wiederholz, has 20 lb (9 kg) pike to his credit said: 'I don't know why it is, but a northern pike lying in shallow water is more likely to charge a large streamer lure than anything else the angler may offer. I've found that such a fly, 5 to 7 in (12–17 cm) long, is deadlier on pike than any surface or underwater plug, any popping bug or any spoon—including a red and white striped one.'

Nowadays, there is a revival of the method in Britain, and with it has come a misconception. A lot of anglers are incredulous of 'fly fishing for pike' because they are under the mistaken impression that artificials which imitate insects are used.

This, of course, is not true. Pike rarely rise to insect life—though a 22 lb 12 oz (10·3 kg) specimen did fall for a Hackled Mayfly in the river Erne in 1945—and on the infrequent occasions when they do it is usually to such creatures as dragonflies and butterflies, which I personally believe they take in mistake for small fish. No, fly fishing for pike is purely a lure and wet fly method, more correctly described as 'soft lure wobbling with fly tackle'.

Reservoir equipment is perfectly suitable for this approach. I use a heavy rod which takes a number 9 or 10 shooting-head—a sinker or floater depending on the depth of the water and the way in which I want to present the lure.

All patterns of single-hook and tandem-hook lures appeal to pike, but they need to be tied on hooks fitted with either a thick monofilament tippet or a flexible stranded-wire tippet of about 6 in (15 cm) length, to avoid being severed from the leader by the razor-sharp teeth of these fish. The tippet, 20–25 lb (9–11 kg) strength, is held firmly in place by twisting it along the shank of the hook, smearing it with a quick-dry waterproof adhesive such as Araldite, and binding over with silk thread or fine copper wire while still tacky. The pattern of the fly is then dressed on in the normal way.

The leader consists of a level length of 20 lb (9 kg) monofilament, needle-knotted to the fly-line and eyed at the free end. A lure fitted with a wire tippet is secured by passing the end of the tippet through the eye and twisting it back four or five times round its length. A lure fitted with a mono-filament tippet is secured with a tucked half-blood knot.

Construction of pike-lure tippet

thick monofilament or soft stranded wire

6 inches (15 cm)

fix tippet with quick-dry adhesive

bind over with silk thread or fine copper wire

A pike lure— and rudd fry spewed-up by a pike that it caught (*Peter Wheat*)

Fly fishing for pike can be tried on waters of all types. It is an interesting method for summer days when pike are at peak fitness and constantly chasing small fish. And in winter, the method can be even more rewarding for big still-water pike gorging themselves on small rudd and such like. The pike charge through the feed-fish in shallow areas, sending them skipping this way and that through the surface, and then follow them up in belly-flopping 'rises'. I took my largest fly-caught pike, a 17 lb 8 oz (7·95 kg) fish, from a Hampshire lake during just such a feeding spree, and the strength of its fight was an experience quite unforgettable.

Pike take lures firmly, but it pays to strike several

Zander

times to make absolutely sure that the hook has penetrated past its barb.

Lures can also be tried for zander, *Stizostedion luciperca*, which are avid eaters of small fish. This species is limited in distribution to a few lakes, canals and slow rivers in England, but where found is well established.

Among coarse species *occasionally* caught on artificial fly, barbel and carp are deserving of special mention.

The Barbel

Family: CYPRINIDAE   *Barbus barbus*
Distribution: Rivers in England only. Limited stocking in a few lakes and reservoirs.
Quality size: 5 lb (2·2 kg)

Barbel weighing over 12 lb (5·4 kg) have been caught by German anglers deliberately fishing for this species with nymph and lure patterns.

In England, as well as lucky captures such as the Kennet barbel which fell for a Dark Woodcock in 1929 and the Thames barbel which fell for a Black Palmer in 1948, there are a number of confirmed reports of barbel being taken purposely on flies.

During the 1930s, Dr J. C. Mottram did research in this field and recorded *catches* of barbel on tiny

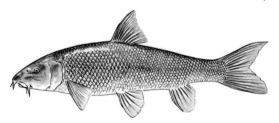

Typical nymph patterns used by German anglers to catch barbel (*Peter Wheat*)

fly-minnows. More recently, Mike Oyez, who manages a 5 acre (2 hectare) gravel-pit fishery stocked with carp and approximately 20 barbel, has reported catching several of these fish on variations of Richard Walker's Hanningfield Lure.

So far, my own random attempts have met with little success, but I keep on trying in the firm conviction that barbel *could* become a regular quarry of fly anglers if only they received more attention than they are getting at the present time.

The Carp

Family CYPRINIDAE   *Cyprinus carpio*
Distribution: Still-waters, slow rivers, and back waters of fast rivers, in all parts of England. Limited distribution in southern Ireland, southern Scotland and Wales.
Quality size: 6 lb (2·7 kg)

Catching carp on artificial flies is nothing like so

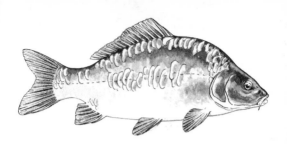

outlandish an activity as dyed-in-the-wool coarse fishermen might suppose. In fact, like fly fishing for pike, it is a very old practice, and in sporting magazines dating from as far back as the early years of the 19th century are to be found remarkable engravings of artificial flies specifically designed for catching carp.

In American lakes it has been found a successful method even for carp weighing over 20 lb (9 kg). And already in Britain there are quite a few anglers with fly-caught carp to their credit, including Gordon Fraser of Melton Mowbray in Leicestershire who, in June 1976, successfully beat an Eye Brook Reservoir specimen estimated to weigh between 25 lb (11 kg) and 30 lb (13 kg). This truly outstanding fish, taken on a size 12 brown nymph to a 5 lb (2·2 kg) leader point, had to be played for over an hour before it was ready for the net.

Carp are inquisitive fish. They habitually patrol the water in search of food, and are as likely to suck in a bait which is on or near the surface as a bait on the bottom. It is this willingness to feed in the upper levels which makes their catching on artificial fly such a feasible proposition.

Providing the water is not too weedy, or so bushed in that casting a fly is impossible except from a boat, it is a straightforward exercise to catch *small* carp with a reservoir rod matched with the lightest line it will handle and a leader tapering to a 6 lb (2·7 kg) point (minimum).

Nymphs and wet flies are worth trying, but bushy all-white floaters tied on size 6 and 8 hooks are the most suitable patterns in my experience. These dry flies resemble no form of natural insect, except perhaps large butterflies or moths, but carp take them happily enough in exactly the same way as they suck down chunks of floating bread!

This is a searching style of carp fishing, the angler moving slowly along the bank looking for fish, and casting only to those which indicate by their movements that they might be interested in a floating bait.

If a breeze is blowing, the fly can be dropped up-wind to drift over the heads of the carp. Evening and dawn are the two periods when these tactics work really well.

Carp weighing less than 8 lb (3·6 kg) are considered small by present-day standards, but on reservoir-strength tackle they fight hard enough to satisfy the needs of any angler.

NOTE: *Restrictions on methods are less severe on coarse-fish-only waters, and this makes possible the priming of the hook with a single white maggot as additional attraction. This 'extra', however, is strictly forbidden on fly-only trout preserves.*

Artificial fly primed with a live maggot

12: FINAL MATTERS

Fishing seasons

Trout and coarse fishing seasons are subject to a great deal of local variation in Britain and Ireland, and detailed information should always be sought as a matter of habit when planning to visit a water located in an unfamiliar area.

Most trout fisheries operate from March or April to September or October. The coarse fishing season for the majority of areas extends from the 16th of June to the 14th of March inclusive.

Periods of the year when fishing is not allowed are known as close seasons—the trout fishing close season and the coarse fishing close season.

Permission to fish

It is against the law to angle for fish without first purchasing a Regional Water Authority Rod Licence covering either trout or coarse fish, or trout and coarse fish combined. This licence, valid for the length of one season or a shorter period, is obtained from a tackle dealer or other agent appointed by the RWA in whose area the water to be fished is situated. It entitles the holder to engage in angling anywhere within the issuing authority's area—providing permission of the person or organization controlling the fishing rights is gained first.

The only fisheries where an individual rod licence is not required are those operating a special general licence covering all visitors to their waters.

A few waters, mainly containing only coarse fish,

are known as 'free waters'. That is to say, they are waters where it is legal to angle without the need for further permission beyond the possession of a rod licence. Usually, however, permission must be paid for in the form of a day, period or season ticket, club subscription or syndicate share.

In nearly all cases, trout fishing permits must be purchased in advance: by post from the owner or his agent, on site from a keeper or manager at a bankside office, or from a self-service ticket dispenser.

Coarse fishing permits are also distributed in these ways but, additionally, some managements allow fishing to start first and the day-ticket permit to be paid for later to a 'collector'—normally a regular bailiff—who visits each angler along the bank. Never assume this to be the system without checking first. If it isn't, the result could be a court appearance. Rules and regulations are printed on rod licences and permits, and on notice-boards in huts, lodges and alongside the water. Read them and obey them. What is perfectly correct drill for one fishery may be absolutely banned somewhere else.

Catch limits

A trout permit usually restricts the holder to catching a set number of fish. When the stated limit is reached, either a second permit is bought or fishing must cease for that day. A few fisheries differ from the norm in this respect. For example, one well-known fishery charges a set sum to fish, *plus 50p more per pound (0·45 kg) of fish caught*. Another fishery has a three-fish bag limit, but allows more fish to be caught and kept *providing they are paid for by the pound (0·45 kg)*.

Hold individual fish on an even keel for photographing

Photographing the catch

Coarse fish must be handled with care when they are being photographed. A catch should be arranged on either a sheet of plastic or an area of short grass which has been liberally soaked with several buckets of water. Large individual specimens are more easily dealt with by holding them gently in wetted hands—but always on an even keel, to prevent possible damage to vital organs. Never grip fish too tightly, rub them against dry clothing, stick fingers under their gill-covers, or keep them out of water longer than is absolutely necessary.

Returning fish

Large hard-fighting coarse fish benefit from being rested in a knotless keepnet before being returned. A short period of confinement allows ample time for the restoration of strength and balance.

To return a big fish, it should be held loosely

Correct method of returning a big fish

between the hands in water just deep enough to cover its back, until it is able to wiggle free under its own power. If returned to running water, a fish must always be positioned with its head facing upstream. *The other way round will kill it.*

Country advice

Do not leave gates open, light open fires, throw away unstubbed cigarette ends, park the car where it will obstruct, disturb animals, damage plant life in any form, or leave litter. Rusty tins, broken bottles, plastic bags and stray lengths of line are proven killers of birds and animals alike.

The Anglers' Co-operative Association

This organization, founded in 1948 by angler and barrister John Eastwood, KC, is a voluntary body fighting water pollution through the common law. Membership subscription of anglers and others interested in conservation of rivers and lakes, is the only means of paying the legal and administrative costs of this vital work.

Not all anglers are members, but all anglers should be. Since its formation, the ACA has fought over 1000 serious cases of pollution—losing but one, and that on a mere technicality. There can be no doubt that the ACA is by far the most successful safeguard we have in the constant battle against those who thoughtlessly and carelessly defile precious water.

For further information write to the ACA, Midland Bank Chambers, Westgate, Grantham, Lincolnshire, NG31 6LE.

Bottom-tackle fly-methods

The controller method enables artificial flies to be fished on ordinary bottom tackle. A suitable outfit consists of a 10–11 ft (3–3·3 m) Avon-action rod, a fixed-spool reel loaded with monofilament strong enough to deal with the conditions and the potential size of the fish, a selection of dry flies, and a controller.

The controller—a streamlined bubble float, a length of swan quill with its open-end blocked off, or a shaped piece of balsa wood varnished to make it waterproof—is a specialized type of float which is attached to the line with long rubber bands at top

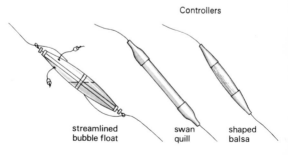

Controllers

streamlined
bubble float

swan
quill

shaped
balsa

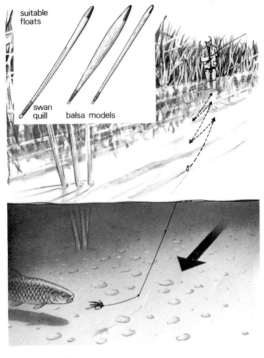

suitable floats

swan quill

balsa models

Float-fishing a fly

and bottom, about 2 ft (60 cm) above the fly. The line is greased to make it float, and the fly is attached by a tucked half-blood knot.

This is mainly a river method for catching bleak, dace, chub and grayling, the tackle being worked with the current in such a way that the fly moves without drag ahead of the controller. This form of presentation is more easily accomplished by wading or boating to a position directly upstream from the controller's path.

The controller is not—as a normal float is—a bite indicator. The strike is made *immediately* the fly is taken, without any delay for the controller to submerge. By taking advantage of surface drift, this rig is also fairly useful for hunting rudd and carp in lakes.

To float-fish a fly for grayling, dace, chub, perch or pike, a *weighted* nymph, wet fly or lure is tied on in place of the bait-hook. The artificial is trotted far downstream slightly above the bottom, and is then slowly zigzagged back upstream by alternately retrieving the float 6 ft (1·8 m) and letting it drop back 3 ft (0·9 m). Bites are indicated by tugs on the rod tip and by the float diving under. A fast strike routine is essential.

A fly is bottom-bumped closely past fish in a clear stream or lake by fixing it to the end of the

Terminal rig for bottom-bumping a fly

split-shot

4 inches (10 cm)

line and weighting it with one, two or three large split-shot. Nymphs, wet flies and lures are all suitable for this method.

NOTE: *These additional methods—perfectly legitimate for catching coarse fish—are not acceptable on fly-only trout waters.*

Fly fishing in the sea

American anglers successfully pursue such fighting sea fish as striped bass, bonefish, tarpon, bluefish and marlin with fly tackle of similar strength to the gear used in Britain for catching reservoir trout.

None of these species swim in British coastal waters, it is true, but other fish are present which could provide regular salt-water fly-sport for British anglers—if only their capture on fly was taken seriously.

I am not suggesting that this is a new approach, because it is nothing of the sort. It has been publicized by different writers for well over 100 years

A typical salmon fly

Durham Ranger

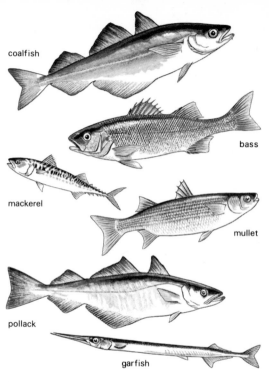

coalfish

bass

mackerel

mullet

pollack

garfish

Saltwater species which respond to fly-fishing methods

as a deadly technique for grey mullet, bass and mackerel. And John Bickerdyke, in his book *Letters to Sea-Fishers* (2nd edition, 1902), devoted a whole chapter to fly-fishing tactics for sea trout, pollack, bass, mackerel, slob trout, coalfish and mullet. He suggested small salmon flies—Durham Ranger, Thunder and Lightning, and Jock Scott—as lures for sea trout and bass, and a fly of his own innovation, the Whitebait Fly, as a sound general pattern for all the species mentioned above.

Estuaries, inlets, tidal pools, sea lochs, harbours and rocky sections of the coastline, are all obvious marks to search with fly tackle—using a fast-sink, slow-sink or wet-tip line according to the conditions and depth of water.

An interesting technique for mackerel during the summer months, when the sea is calm, is to take out a small boat and drift with the tide, casting large bright lures on a sinking line. Early morning and late evening are the best periods for this style of fishing, while the mackerel shoals are close to shore chasing brit. A patch of intense gull activity and brit skittering across the surface is a reliable indication that mackerel are probably feeding below. The aim then is to direct the drift to bring the boat through the disturbed area.

Mackerel are extremely simple to hook once they have been located, but though they average less than 1 lb (0·45 kg), they fight with so much vigour that to play them on fly-tackle feels like being attached to fish several times their weight.

Bass, pollack and garfish are other species which fall for this method.

All items of tackle should be thoroughly washed with fresh water to prevent corrosion. This should be done as soon after the end of a sea trip as possible, and certainly never later than the same day.

Old tackle discarded for freshwater fishing is ideal for fly fishing in the sea.

NOTE: Veniard's publish a booklet of fly dressings recommended for sea fishing.

Dapping with natural flies

This is a technique with which I am not personally familiar, but which I know is practised with considerable success by anglers drift-fishing the large limestone lakes of Ireland such as Corrib, Derg and Conn.

A very long rod is used, matched with a special silk floss line which is so light and delicate that it is easily lifted by the softest breeze. At the end of the leader a large hook is tied on, and to this hook a bunch of natural insects is impaled.

By holding the rod high, the wind is able to catch the line and billow it far out in advance of the boat's drift. The angler then manipulates the tackle to dibble the bait on the surface as neatly as possible.

The two principal periods of the year when this ancient style of fishing is exceptionally productive occur during May–June when there are heavy hatches of mayfly, and late summer when large numbers of crane-flies are falling on the water.

Dragonflies, grasshoppers and big bushy dry flies are also fished 'on the dap'.

Salmon fishing

Salmon enter sea-connected river systems during the weeks between spring and autumn. These powerful fish range in size from a few pounds to 60 lb plus (27 kg), and being at peak fitness following months of rich feeding in marine conditions they offer superb sport on rod and line.

Although salmon do not feed in fresh water, or only rarely so, as they journey upstream to their gravelly spawning sites, they can be 'teased' to take a gob of worms, a prawn, a spinner, a plug, a small fish mounted on a spinning flight, or an artificial fly.

Rivers which receive good runs of salmon are few and far between, and, though inexpensive day-ticket salmon fishing is available in some areas, the better-class beats are all strictly preserved and only to be fished at enormous cost. Hence the fact that catching a salmon on fly is rather an uncommon, or even unknown, experience for the majority of anglers.

Salmon are fly-caught (particularly fish of smaller size) on ordinary reservoir-strength trout gear. Regular salmon anglers, however, also include in their tackle longer rods (some designed for two-handed casting), larger reels, heavier lines, stouter leaders, and flies much bigger on average than those normally employed for trout and coarse fish, other than pike.

Generally speaking, unless access is readily available to a first-class stretch of water, the beginner is unlikely to be able to practise fly fishing for salmon with any real chance of success. And certainly never often enough to warrant the outlay involved in obtaining pukka salmon tackle.

Books for Further Reading

Natural History

Life in Lakes and Rivers (1951) by T. T. Macan and
E. B. Worthington. Collins

British Freshwater Fishes (1967) by M. E. Varley.
Fishing News (Books) Ltd

The Trout (1967) by W. E. Frost and M. E. Brown.
Collins

An Angler's Entomology (1956) by J. R. Harris.
Collins

Trout Fly Recognition (1971) by John Goddard.
A. & C. Black

Trout Flies of Stillwater (1975) by John Goddard.
A. & C. Black

The Observer's Book of Freshwater Fishes (Revised 1970)
by T. B. Bagenal. Warne

The Observer's Book of Sea Fishes (1972) by T. B.
Bagenal. Warne

Fly Tying

Fly-Tying Illustrated (1976) by Freddie Rice. David
& Charles

Fly Tying for Beginners (1974) by Geoffrey Bucknall.
Benn

Fly Dressers' Guide (1970) by John Veniard. A. & C.
Black

Fly-Dressing (1976) by David J. Collyer. David &
Charles

A Further Guide to Fly Dressing (1972) by John
Veniard. A. & C. Black

A Reference Book of English Trout Flies (1967) by
W. H. Lawrie. Pelham

A Dictionary of Trout Flies (1973) by A. Courtney-Williams. A. & C. Black

Fly Dressing Innovations (1974) by Richard Walker. Benn

Reservoir and Lake Flies (1970) compiled by John Veniard. A. & C. Black

Rough Stream Trout Flies (1976) by S. D. Price. A. & C. Black

Tackle and Casting

The Truth About Tackle by Dermot Wilson. Nether Wallop Mill, Hampshire

Rod Building (1975) by A. Vare and K. Whitehead. Rod & Gun Publishing Ltd

Tactics

Presenting The Fly to the Trout (1967) by Frederick E. Mold. Herbert Jenkins

Fishing The Dry Fly (1970) by Dermot Wilson. A. & C. Black

Nymphs and The Trout (1970) by Frank Sawyer. A. & C. Black

Grayling (1968) by R. V. Righyni. Macdonald & Jane's

Stillwater Fly Fishing (1975) by T. C. Ivens. André Deutsch

Bank Fishing for Reservoir Trout (1972) by Jim Calver. A. & C. Black

Catch More Stillwater Trout (1975) by Bob Church. Wolfe Publishing

Reservoir Trout Fishing (1968) by Geoffrey Bucknall. Pelham

Waters

Where to Fish. Published annually by 'The Field'

Fishing Waters. Compiled by Bill Howes. Published annually by Link House Publications

Stillwater Trout Fisheries (1976). Edited by H. F. Wallis. Benn

Legal

Angling and The Law (1974) by Michael Gregory. Charles Knight

Books by Peter Wheat

The Observer's Book of Coarse Fishing (1976). Warne

The Fighting Barbel (1967). Benn

Improve Your Coarse Angling (1967). Davies Books

Fishing As We Find It (1997). Warne (Edited)

Popular Sea Fishing (1968). Warne (Edited)

The Angler's Year 1971. Pelham (Edited)

The Angler's Year 1972. Pelham (Edited)

Pelham Manual of River Coarse Fishing (1968). Pelham

Catch More Dace (1975). Wolfe Publishing

Useful Addresses

Mail-Order Tackle and Accessories Service: Dermot Wilson, Nether Wallop Mill, near Stockbridge, Hampshire. SO20 8ES

Rod-Making Materials: J. B. Walker (Fishing Tackle) Ltd, 7 Marine Walk St, Hythe, Kent. CT21 5NP; Simpsons of Turnford, Nunsbury Drive, Turnford, Broxbourne, Hertfordshire.

Fly-Tying Materials: E. Veniard, Paramount Warehouses, 138 Northwood Rd, Thornton Heath, Surrey. CR4 8YG

A SELECTION OF DAY-TICKET TROUT WATERS IN ENGLAND AND WALES

England

Avon

Barrow Gurney Reservoirs, nr Bristol. Numbers 2 and 3 totalling 65 acres (26 ha). Boats.

Blagdon Reservoir, nr Bristol. 450 acres (182 ha). Boats.

Cameley Trout Lakes, nr Bristol. 4 acres (1·8 ha).

Chew Valley Lake, nr Bristol. 1210 acres (489 ha). Boats.

Berkshire

Black Swan Lake, Dinton Pastures, Hurst St Nicholas, nr Reading. 75 acres (30 ha).

Datchet Reservoir, nr Windsor. 480 acres (194 ha). Boat fishing only.

Buckinghamshire

Latimer Park Lakes, nr Chesham. Two lakes totalling 13 acres (5 ha), plus stretch of river Chess. Boats.

Cambridgeshire

Chatteris Aqua Sports, Block Fen, nr Mepal. 25 acres (10 ha). Boats.

Grafham Water, St Neots. 1670 acres (676 ha). Boats.

Cheshire

Lamaload Reservoir, nr Macclesfield. 70 acres (28 ha).

Cleveland

Tees Valley Reservoirs, upper Teesdale. Comprising Balderhead 280 acres (113 ha), Selset 270 acres (109 ha), Cowgreen 280 acres (113 ha), Scaling Dam 140 acres (56 ha), Lockwood Beck 34 acres (13 ha), Grasholme, Hury and Blackton. Boats.

Cornwall

Argal Reservoir, nr Penryn. 65 acres (26 ha). Boats.

College Reservoir, nr Penryn. 38 acres (15 ha).

Crowdy Reservoir, nr Camelford. 115 acres (46 ha).

Drift Reservoir, nr Penzance. 64 acres (24 ha).

Porth Reservoir, nr Newquay. 40 acres (16 ha). Boats.

Siblyback Reservoir, nr Liskeard. 140 acres (56 ha). Boats.

Stithians Reservoir, nr Redruth. 274 acres (110 ha).

Tamar Lake, nr Bude. 51 acres (20 ha).

Upper Tamar Reservoir, nr Bude. 81 acres (32 ha). Boats.

Cumbria

Bigland Hall Trout Fishery, nr Newby Bridge. 16 acres (6 ha).

Derbyshire

Higham Farm, nr Alfreton. Four lakes totalling 12 acres (5 ha), plus 1½ miles (2·4 km) of river Amber. Day-tickets only to residents of Higham Farm Hotel.

Ladybower Reservoir, nr Bamford. 500 acres (202 ha).

Linacre Reservoirs, nr Chesterfield. Two waters totalling 25 acres (10 ha).

Ogston Reservoir, nr Alfreton. 206 acres (83 ha).

Devon

Avon Dam Reservoir, nr South Brent. 50 acres (20 ha).

Burrator Reservoir, Yelverton, nr Plymouth. 150 acres (60 ha). Boats.

Dart Raffe Lake, nr Witheridge. 2 acres (0·8 ha). Boats.

Fernworthy Reservoir. Chagford. 76 acres (30 ha). Boats.

Harcombe House Fishery, Chudleigh. Three lakes totalling 5 acres (2 ha).

Kennick Reservoir, nr Newton Abbot. 45 acres (18 ha).

Little Comfort Farm, nr Braunton. 1 acre (0·4 ha).

Meldon Reservoir, nr Okehampton. 54 acres (21 ha).

Slade Reservoir, nr Ilfracombe. Two waters totalling 10 acres (4 ha).

Stafford Moor Fishery, Dolton, Winkleigh. 14 acres (5 ha).

Tottiford Reservoir, nr Newton Abbot. 35 acres (14 ha).

Wistlandpound Reservoir, nr Barnstaple. 41 acres (16 ha).

Durham

Derwent Reservoir, Edmundbyers, nr Consett. 1000 acres (404 ha). Boats.

East Sussex

Darwell Reservoir, Mountfield, nr Battle. 180 acres (72 ha). Boats.

Great Sanders Reservoir, nr Sedlescombe. 54 acres (21 ha). Boats.

Essex

Ardleigh Reservoir, nr Colchester. 130 acres (52 ha). Boats.

East Hanningfield Hall, East Hanningfield, nr Chelmsford. 2 acres (0·8 ha).

Gloucestershire
Ampney Park Fishery, Ampney Crucis, nr Cirencester. Lake of 2½ acres (1 ha), plus short stretch of river. Boat.

Greater London
Kempton Park West Reservoir, nr Hanworth. 20 acres (8 ha).
Walthamstow No. 1. Reservoir, Ferry Lane, Walthamstow. 20 acres (8 ha).

Greater Manchester
Upper Rivington Reservoir, Bolton.
Upper Roddlesworth Reservoir, Bolton.

Hampshire
Allens Farm, Sandleheath, Fordingbridge. Four lakes totalling 6 acres (2 ha), plus ½ mile (0·8 km) of river.
Alre Fishery, Fob Down, Alresford. Two waters totalling 1½ acres (0·2 ha), plus 1 mile (1·6 km) stretch of river Alre.
Avington Trout Fishery, nr Winchester. Three lakes totalling 8 acres (3 ha), plus ¾ mile (1 km) of river Itchen.
Bagwell Green, Winchfield, nr Basingstoke. Two lakes totalling 2 acres (0·8 ha).
Botleigh Grange Hotel Lakes, Hedge End, Botley, nr Southampton. Two lakes.
Damerham Trout Lakes, Damerham, nr Fordingbridge. Six lakes totalling 17 acres (7 ha).
Horns Farm Trout Fishery, Lower Common, Eversley, nr Basingstoke. 5 acres (2 ha).

Leominsted Trout Fishery, Emery Down, nr
Lyndhurst. 8 acres (3 ha).

Hertfordshire
Oughton Fishery, Burford Ray Lodge, Bedford
Road, Hitchin. 2 acres (0·8 ha).
Netherhall Fishery, Hoddesdon. 5 acres (2 ha).

Kent
Pooh Corner Fishery, Rolvenden, Cranbrook. 1 acre
(0·4 ha).
Tenterden Trout Fishery, Tenterden.

Lancashire
Barnsfold Reservoirs, nr Goosnargh, Preston. Two
waters totalling 20 acres (8 ha). Boats.

Leicestershire
Eye Brook Reservoir, Caldecott, Uppingham. 400
acres (161 ha). Boats.
Kirby Bellars Lake, Melton Mowbray. 17 acres
(7 ha).
Rutland Water, nr Oakham. 3100 acres (1254 ha).
Boats.
Thornton Reservoir, Loughborough. 76 acres (30
ha). Boats.

Lincolnshire
Hillview Lake, Hogsthorpe, nr Skegness. $1\frac{1}{2}$ acres
(0.6 ha).
Swansholme Park, Lincoln Fisheries, Doddington
Road, Lincoln. Two lakes totalling 20 acres
(8 ha). Boats.
Toft Newton Reservoir, nr Market Rasen. 40 acres
(16 ha).

North Yorkshire

Cod Beck Reservoir, nr Northallerton.

Malham Tarn, Settle. Boats.

The Haven, Long Marston, nr Wetherby. $1\frac{1}{2}$ acres (0·6 ha).

Northamptonshire

Elinor Fishery, Aldwincle, nr Thrapston. Two waters totalling 36 acres (14 ha). Punts.

Pitsford Reservoir, nr Northampton. 739 acres (299 ha). Boats.

Ravensthorpe Reservoir, nr Northampton. 114 acres (46 ha). Boats.

Nottinghamshire

Colwick Trout Fishery, Colwick, nr Nottingham. 11 acres (4 ha).

Cromwell Lake, nr Newark. 20 acres (8 ha).

Oxfordshire

Linch Hill Fishery, Stanton Harcourt. 58 acres (23 ha). Boats.

Somerset

Clatworthy Reservoir, nr Taunton. 130 acres (52 ha). Boats.

Durleigh Reservoir, nr Bridgwater. 77 acres (31 ha). Boats.

Exe Valley Fishery, Dulverton. Two ponds totalling $1\frac{1}{4}$ acres (0·5 ha).

Hawkridge Reservoir, nr Bridgwater. 32 acres (12 ha).

Otterhead Lakes, Churchingford, nr Taunton. Two linked lakes totalling $4\frac{1}{2}$ acres (1·8 ha).

Sutton Bingham Reservoir, nr Yeovil. 142 acres (57 ha). Boats.

South Yorkshire

Dam Flask Reservoir, Low Bradfield, nr Sheffield.

Ladybower Reservoir, nr Sheffield. 504 acres (203 ha).

Lindholme Lake, Sandtoft, nr Doncaster. 18 acres (7 ha).

Morehall Reservoir, Bolsterstone, nr Sheffield.

Scout Dike Reservoir, nr Penistone, Sheffield.

Underbank Reservoir, Stocksbridge, nr Sheffield.

Staffordshire

Hamps Valley Fisheries, Winkhill, nr Leek. Two lakes totalling 2 acres (0·8 ha), plus short stretch of river.

Tittesworth Reservoir, nr Leek. 190 acres (76 ha). Boats.

Surrey

Waggoners Wells, lake nr Hindhead.

Willinghurst Trout Fishery, Shamley Green, nr Guildford. Two lakes totalling 4½ acres (1·8 ha).

Winkworth Arboretum, nr Godalming. Two small lakes. Boats.

Tyne and Wear

Whittle Dean Reservoirs, Newcastle. Six waters totalling 108 acres (43 ha).

West Midlands

Draycote Water, nr Rugby. 600 acres (242 ha). Boats.

Packington Estate Fisheries, Meriden. Lake complex totalling 120 acres (48 ha), plus 5 miles (8 km) of river. Boats.

Shustoke Reservoirs, nr Coleshill. Two reservoirs totalling 90 acres (36 ha). Boats.

West Sussex

Boringwheel Fishery, nr Nutley. 6 acres (2·4 ha).

Peckhams Copse, North Mundham, nr Chichester. Two lakes totalling 40 acres (16 ha).

Weir Wood Reservoir, Forest Row, nr East Grinstead. 280 acres (113 ha). Boats.

West Yorkshire

Cromwell Lake, Wakefield Road, Brighouse. 35 acres (14 ha). Boats.

Fewston and Swinsty Reservoirs, Otley. Two adjoining waters.

Thruscross Reservoir, nr Otley. 360 acres (144 ha).

Wiltshire

Brimclose, Fovant, nr Wilton. Two lakes, plus 1¼ miles (2 km) of river.

Wolverton Fishery, Wolverton Zeals, Warminster. 1 acre (0·4 ha).

Wroughton Reservoir, nr Swindon. 2¾ acres (1·1 ha). Punt.

Wales

Clwyd

Alwen Reservoir, nr Denbigh. 368 acres (151 ha).

Cambrian Fisheries, Afonwen. 18 acres (7 ha). Boats.

Dyfed

Dinas Reservoir, nr Aberystwyth. 60 acres (23 ha). Boats.

Llyn Egnant and Teifi Pools, nr Tregaron.

Llyn Glandwgan, Aberystwyth.

Llys-y-Fran Reservoir, nr Maenclochog. 197 acres (79 ha). Boats.

Nant-y-Moch, nr Aberystwyth. 680 acres (275 ha).

Rosebush Reservoir, Maenclochog. 39 acres (15 ha).

Upper Lleidi Reservoir, nr Llanelli. 35 acres (14 ha). Boats.

West Orielton Farm Fisheries, Pembroke. 16 acres (6 ha).

Glamorgan (Mid, South and West Glamorgan)

Cwm Taff Fawr Reservoirs, nr Merthyr Tydfil, Mid Glamorgan. Three waters comprising Beacons 52 acres (21 ha), Cwm Taff 42 acres (17 ha), Llyn Onn 150 acres (60 ha).

Eglwys Nunydd Reservoir, Margam, Port Talbot, West Glamorgan. 250 acres (101 ha).

Lisvane Reservoir, nr Cardiff. 20 acres (8 ha).

Llanishen Reservoir, nr Cardiff. 20 acres (8 ha).

Taf Fechan Reservoirs, nr Merthyr Tydfil, Mid Glamorgan.

Ystrad Fellte Reservoir, nr Merthyr Tydfil, Mid Glamorgan. 59 acres (23 ha).

Gwent

Llandegfedd Reservoir, nr Pontypool. 440 acres (178 ha). Boats.

Wentwood Reservoirs, nr Newport. 40 acres (16 ha). Boats.

Ynysfro and Pantyreas Reservoirs, nr Newport. Two waters totalling 26 acres (10 ha).

Gwynedd

Cefni Reservoir, Llangefni.

Crafnant Lake, nr Llanrwst. Trefriw.

Llyn Alaw, Llangefni. 777 acres (314 ha). Boats.

Llyn Celyn, nr Bala. 1000 acres (404 ha). Boats.

Llyn Padarn, nr Llanberis. 170 acres (68 ha).

Tan-y-Grisiau Reservoir, nr Cynfel. 95 acres (38 ha).

Powys

Clywedog Reservoir, Llanidloes. 600 acres (242 ha). Boats.

Cray Reservoir, nr Sennybridge, Brecon. 100 acres (40 ha).

Elan Estate, nr Rhayader. Streams, lakes and reservoirs.

Fachwen Pool, Aberhafesp. 14 acres (6 ha).

Lake Vyrnwy, nr Llanwddyn. Boats.

Talybont Reservoir, Talybont on Usk, nr Brecon. 318 acres (128 ha). Boats.

Usk Reservoir, nr Trecastle, 290 acres (117 ha). Boats.

Before planning to visit a water, it is advisable first to seek more detailed information regarding opening and closing dates and ticket distribution. Some waters operate an 'on site' system, where tickets can be obtained easily from wardens or self-service machines on the day of fishing, but many others, particularly smaller fisheries with only limited space, are usually so heavily booked that it is always necessary to book ahead by phone or letter to avoid the disappointment of finding on arrival that the daily quota of tickets has already been taken up.

As well as the listed waters, many more day-ticket and club subscription lakes and river stretches in England and Wales are preserved for trout fishing. Local inquiry will discover their locations.

Top class fly-only river trouting in southern England is generally expensive, most of it held strictly for members of clubs and syndicates, and residents of hotels controlling the waters.

An abundance of reasonably-priced day-ticket trouting, stream and lake, is available in Scotland and Ireland, where these fish predominate in waters great and small.

Index

191